## Social Studies

# myWorld
# ACTIVITY GUIDE
## 1

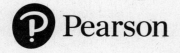

**Boston, Massachusetts**    **Chandler, Arizona**
**Glenview, Illinois**    **New York, New York**

This work is solely for the use of instructors and administrators for the purpose of teaching courses and assessing student learning. Unauthorized dissemination, publication or sale of the work, in whole or in part (including posting on the Internet) will destroy the integrity of the work and is strictly prohibited.

Copyright © 2019 Pearson Education, Inc., or its affiliates. All Rights Reserved. Printed in the United States of America. This publication is protected by copyright, and permission should be obtained from the publisher prior to any prohibited reproduction, storage in a retrieval system, or transmission to any form or in any means, electronic, mechanical, photocopying, recording, or likewise. For information regarding permissions, write to Rights Management & Contracts, Pearson Education, Inc., 221 River Street, Hoboken, New Jersey 07030.

Pearson is a trademark, in the U. S. or other countries, of Pearson Education, Inc., or its affiliates.

ISBN-13: 978-0-328-97314-9
ISBN-10: 0-328-97314-9

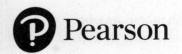

# Contents

© Pearson Education, Inc., All Rights Reserved

# Chapter 4

# Chapter 5

# Chapter 6

© Pearson Education, Inc., All Rights Reserved

# Graphic Organizers

© Pearson Education, Inc., All Rights Reserved

# How to Use This Book

The *myWorld Activity Guide* was designed for teachers who love social studies but want to teach it in a different way. The program focuses on key topics in social studies, aligning to content frequently taught in each grade from Kindergarten to grade 5. The chapters in this book introduce students to social studies through fun activities and engaging inquiries. You can use the Activity Guide on its own, with associated support materials, or in connection with your basal program.

## Teacher Planner

The Chapter Planner outlines the chapter's content in a clear chart with this information:

- **Description** gives a quick overview of each activity and its steps

- **Duration** offers a time estimate, making it easy to plan

- **Materials** lists the materials you will need for each part of the lesson

- **Participants** suggests whether to complete each part of the activity as whole class, small group, or individual

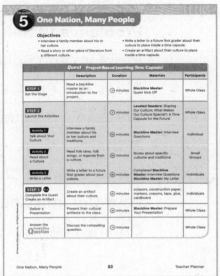

## Quest

Each chapter includes detailed lesson suggestions for a long-term inquiry, or Quest.

- Each Quest starts with a Compelling Question, designed to engage students in the inquiry.

- The Quest is set up with three steps: Set the Stage, Launch the Activities, and Complete the Quest.

- Within each step, you'll find suggestions for guiding students to complete a series of activities, culminating in a final product, such as a hands-on project, presentation, civic discussion, or writing project.

- Each chapter contains suggestions for modifying the activities for English Learners.

- Where appropriate, student worksheets are provided to support student completion of the Quest.

- Rubrics in the front of the book will help you and your students evaluate their work.

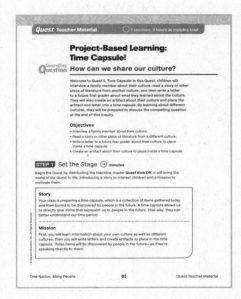

© Pearson Education, Inc., All Rights Reserved

## Quick Activities

Each chapter includes detailed lesson suggestions for a series of short activities related to the chapter content. Where appropriate, student worksheets are provided to support student completion of activities. Rubrics in the front of this book will help you and your students evaluate their work on each activity. The Activity Guide also offers suggestions for modifying the activities for English Learners.

**Examples of Quick Activities are:**

| | |
|---|---|
| Games | Preparing and Acting Out a Skit |
| Debates | Building a Social Media Profile |
| Art Projects | Map Activities |

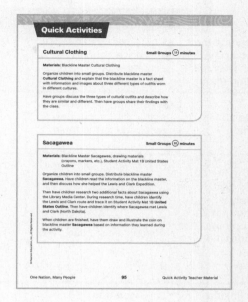

## Read Aloud or Readers Theater

Each chapter has a Read Aloud or Readers Theater related to chapter content. With grade-appropriate language, the stories and Readers Theaters bring to life important content related to the chapter.

## Graphic Organizers

You will find a wide variety of graphic organizers at the back of this book. You will find many uses for them as your students complete the activities and Quests described in this book.

© Pearson Education, Inc., All Rights Reserved

# Opinion Writing

**Directions:** Copy the rubric for individuals or groups (for collaborative writing projects). Rank individuals or groups for each skill. For Grade K, allow students to use a combination of drawing, dictating, and writing to compose their opinion pieces.

| | 4 Excellent | 3 Very Good | 2 Satisfactory | 1 Needs Improvement |
|---|---|---|---|---|
| **Introduce the topic or the book they are writing about.** | • The topic is clearly introduced and is accurate. | • The topic is introduced and is mostly accurate. | • An attempt is made to introduce the topic, but it is incorrect and/or unclear. | • The topic is not introduced. |
| **State an opinion.** | • An opinion is clearly stated and accurately responds to the topic. | • An opinion that mostly responds to the topic is stated but is vague. | • An attempt is made to state an opinion, but it does not respond to the topic and/or is unclear. | • An opinion is not stated. |
| **Supply a reason for the opinion. (Grades 1–2)** | • One reason that clearly supports the opinion is supplied. (G1)<br>• More than one reason that clearly supports the opinion is supplied. (G2) | • One reason that mostly supports the opinion is supplied. (G1)<br>• Only one reason is supplied or more than one reason is supplied, but the reasons mostly support the opinion. (G2) | • An attempt is made to supply a reason, but the reason is either unclear or does not support the opinion. | • No reasons are supplied. |
| **Use linking words (such as *because*, *and*, *or* and *also*) to connect opinion and reasons. (Grade 2)** | • Linking words consistently are used correctly to connect the opinion and reasons. | • Linking words are generally used correctly to connect the opinion and reasons. | • Linking words are used incorrectly to connect the opinion and reasons. | • Linking words are not used to connect the opinion and reasons. |
| **Provide some sense of closure. (Grade 1)** | • Closure is provided by restating the opinion without introducing new ideas. | • Closure is provided by restating the opinion, but the restatement either introduces new ideas or is vague. | • A minimal sense of closure is provided with a vague restatement of the opinion and the introduction of new ideas. | • Closure is not provided. |
| **Provide a concluding statement or section. (Grade 2)** | • A concluding statement or section is provided and includes a clear restatement of the opinion without introducing new ideas. | • A concluding statement or section is provided, but it includes a vague restatement of the opinion or introduces new ideas. | • An attempt is made to provide a concluding statement or section, but it includes a vague restatement of the opinion and new ideas. | • A concluding statement or section is not provided. |

© Pearson Education, Inc., All Rights Reserved

# Informative/Explanatory Writing

**Directions:** Copy the rubric for individuals or groups (for collaborative writing projects). Rank individuals or groups for each skill. For Grade K, allow students to use a combination of drawing, dictating, and writing to compose their Informative/explanatory texts.

| | 4 Excellent | 3 Good | 2 Satisfactory | 1 Needs Improvement |
|---|---|---|---|---|
| **Name or introduce the topic.** | • The topic is clearly and correctly named. (Grades K–1)<br>• The topic is clearly and correctly introduced. (Grade 2) | • The topic is correctly named but is vague. (Grades K–1)<br>• The topic is correctly introduced but is vague. (Grade 2) | • An attempt is made to name the topic but is incorrect and unclear. (Grades K–1)<br>• An attempt is made to introduce the topic but is incorrect and unclear. (Grade 2) | • The topic is not named. (Grades K–1)<br>• The topic is not introduced. (Grade 2) |
| **Supply information or facts about the topic. (Grades K–1)** | • Information (Grade K) or facts (Grade 1) clearly about the topic are supplied. | • Some information (Grade K) or facts (Grade 1) that are mostly about the topic are supplied. | • An attempt is made to supply information (Grade K) or facts (Grade 1), but the information/facts are either unclear or not about the topic. | • No information (Grade K) or facts (Grade 1) about the topic are provided. |
| **Use facts and definitions to develop points. (Grade 2)** | • Facts and definitions are used effectively to develop points. | • Some facts and definitions are used to develop points. | • Facts and definitions are used but are not effective in developing points. | • No facts and definitions are used to develop points. |
| **Provide some sense of closure. (Grade 1)** | • Closure is provided by restating the topic without introducing new ideas. | • Closure is provided by restating the topic, but the restatement either introduces new ideas or is vague. | • A minimal sense of closure is provided with a vague restatement of the topic and the introduction of new ideas. | • Closure is not provided. |
| **Provide a concluding statement or section. (Grade 2)** | • A concluding statement or section is provided and includes a clear restatement of the topic without introducing new ideas. | • A concluding statement or section is provided, but it includes a vague restatement of the topic or introduces new ideas. | • An attempt is made to provide a concluding statement or section, but it includes a vague restatement of the topic and new ideas. | • A concluding statement or section is not provided. |

© Pearson Education, Inc., All Rights Reserved

# Narrative Writing

**Directions:** Copy the rubric for individuals or groups (for collaborative writing projects). Rank individuals or groups for each skill. For Grade K, allow students to use a combination of drawing, dictating, and writing to compose their narratives.

| | **4** Excellent | **3** Very Good | **2** Satisfactory | **1** Needs Improvement |
|---|---|---|---|---|
| **Recount two or more events in appropriate sequence.** | • Two or more events are clearly recounted in an appropriate sequence. | • Two or more events are recounted, but the appropriate sequence is unclear. | • Two or more events are recounted, but the sequence is incorrect and unclear or only one event is recounted. | • No events are recounted. |
| **Provide a reaction to what happened. (Grade K only)** | • A clear reaction to what happened is provided. | • A reaction to what happened is provided but is unclear. | • A reaction is provided, but it is unrelated to what happened. | • A reaction to what happened is not provided. |
| **Include details. (Grades 1–2)** | • Specific details regarding what happened are included. | • Details regarding what happened are included, but some important details are vague. | • Details regarding what happened are included, but some important details are vague and others are missing. | • No details are included. |
| **Use temporal words to signal event order. (Grades 1–2)** | • Temporal words are used consistently and accurately to signal event order. | • Temporal words are sometimes used to accurately signal event order. | • Temporal words are occasionally used to signal event order and may be used inaccurately. | • Temporal words are not used. |
| **Provide a sense of closure. (Grades 1–2)** | • A strong sense of closure is provided with a clear ending. | • A sense of closure is provided with a vague ending. | • An attempt is made to provide closure with an ending that trails off. | • No sense of closure is provided. |

© Pearson Education, Inc., All Rights Reserved

# Project-Based Learning

**Directions:** Copy the rubric for individuals or groups. Rank individuals or groups for each skill as they participate in shared research to complete an inquiry project.

| | 4 Excellent | 3 Good | 2 Satisfactory | 1 Needs Improvement |
|---|---|---|---|---|
| **PLAN THE INQUIRY:** Collaborate to develop a project plan. | • Assigns and accepts tasks within the group, encouraging all group members to play a role and contribute equally. <br>• Participates fully in collaborative conversations with partners about the inquiry for the duration of the project and follows agreed-upon rules for discussion. <br>• Participates fully in identifying details of the final outcome. | • Accepts tasks within the group, generally encouraging group members to play a role and contribute equally. <br>• Participates in collaborative conversations with partners about the inquiry and generally follows agreed-upon rules for discussion. <br>• Participates in identifying the details for the final outcome. | • Sometimes accepts tasks within the group, occasionally encouraging group members to play a role and contribute equally. <br>• Sometimes participates in collaborative conversations with partners about the inquiry and may need occasional reminders to follow the agreed-upon rules for discussion. <br>• Participates somewhat in identifying the details for the final outcome. | • Rarely accepts tasks within the group or encourages group members to play a role and contribute equally. <br>• Rarely participates in collaborative conversations with partners about the inquiry and rarely follows agreed-upon rules for discussion. <br>• Does not participate in identifying the details for the final outcome. |
| **DO YOUR RESEARCH:** Find sources to support your inquiry. | • Finds relevant evidence in support of own interpretations. <br>• Routinely asks and answers questions about key details to clarify meaning. <br>• Reads or explores a number of sources to gain, modify, or extend knowledge or to learn different perspectives. <br>• Always synthesizes and draws conclusions from information acquired through research. | • Generally finds relevant evidence in support of own interpretations. <br>• Usually asks and answers questions about key details to clarify meaning. <br>• Reads or explores at least one source to gain, modify, or extend knowledge or to learn different perspectives. <br>• Generally synthesizes and draws conclusions from information acquired through research. | • Finds some evidence in support of own interpretations, but it may be irrelevant. <br>• Occasionally asks and answers questions about key details to clarify meaning. <br>• Attempts to read or explore sources but struggles to gain, modify, or extend knowledge. <br>• Attempts to synthesize and draw conclusions from information acquired through research, but conclusions are vague. | • Finds little or no evidence in support of own interpretations. <br>• Rarely or never asks and answers questions about key details to clarify or determine meaning. <br>• Does not attempt to read or explore sources to gain, modify, or extend knowledge. <br>• Does not synthesize or draw conclusions from information acquired through research. |
| **PRODUCE THE PRODUCT:** Demonstrate understanding of key ideas. | • Expresses understanding of new concepts while creating the product. <br>• Consistently uses language acquired from research in speaking and writing about the product. <br>• Adds multiple visuals to enhance the product. | • Generally expresses understanding of new concepts while creating the product. <br>• Generally uses language acquired from research in speaking and writing about the product. <br>• Adds at least one visual to enhance the product. | • Occasionally expresses understanding of new concepts while creating the product. <br>• Occasionally uses language acquired from research in speaking and writing about the product. <br>• Adds a visual, but it is irrelevant and does not enhance the product. | • Rarely expresses understanding of new concepts while creating the product. <br>• Rarely uses language acquired from research in speaking and writing about the product. <br>• Does not include a visual. |
| **REFLECT ON THE INQUIRY:** Discuss the Compelling Question. | • Fully articulates a meaningful response to the Compelling Question. | • Generally articulates a meaningful response to the Compelling Question. | • Attempts to articulate a response to the Compelling Question, but the response is vague or irrelevant. | • Does not attempt to respond to the Compelling Question. |

© Pearson Education, Inc., All Rights Reserved

# Shared Discussion

**Directions:** Copy the rubric for individuals, pairs, or groups as they participate in collaborative discussions with diverse partners about grade-appropriate topics and texts. Rank individuals or groups for each skill.

|  | 4 Excellent | 3 Good | 2 Satisfactory | 1 Needs Improvement |
|---|---|---|---|---|
| **Follow agreed-upon rules for discussions.** | • Follows agreed-upon rules at all times.<br>• Consistently uses deliberative processes when making group decisions. | • Follows agreed-upon rules most of the time.<br>• Generally uses deliberative processes when making group decisions. | • Follows agreed-upon rules sometimes, but needs occasional direction.<br>• Sometimes uses deliberative processes when making group decisions. | • Does not follow agreed-upon rules without teacher direction.<br>• Does not use deliberative processes when making group decisions. |
| **Ask and answer questions and respond to others.** | • Consistently asks and answers questions to clarify something that is not understood.<br>• Consistently asks questions to clear up confusion about the topics or texts under discussion. (Grades 1–2)<br>• Consistently builds on others' talk in conversations by responding to comments. (Grades 1–2) | • Often asks and answers questions to clarify something that is not understood.<br>• Often asks questions to clear up confusion about the topics or texts under discussion. (Grades 1–2)<br>• Often builds on others' talk in conversations by responding to comments. (Grades 1–2) | • Attempts to ask and answer questions to clarify something that is not understood.<br>• Attempts to ask questions but is not always successful in clearing up confusion about the topics or texts under discussion. (Grades 1–2)<br>• Attempts to build on others' talk in conversations by responding to comments. (Grades 1–2) | • Rarely if ever asks or answers questions to clarify something that is not understood.<br>• Does not ask questions to clear up confusion about the topics or texts under discussion. (Grades 1–2)<br>• Rarely if ever builds on others' talk in conversations by responding to comments. (Grades 1–2) |
| **Describe people, places, things, and events with relevant details.** | • Thoroughly describes people, places, things, and events with relevant details. | • Generally describes people, places, things, and events with mostly relevant details. | • Attempts to describe people, places, things, and events, but details may be missing or irrelevant. | • Rarely if ever describes people, places, things, or events. |
| **Speak audibly and express thoughts, feelings, and ideas clearly.** | • Always speaks audibly and clearly expresses thoughts, feelings, and ideas. | • Generally speaks audibly and expresses thoughts, feelings, and ideas. | • Attempts to speak audibly and to express thoughts, feelings, and ideas, but is difficult to understand at times. | • Does not speak audibly and does not express thoughts, feelings, and ideas. |

© Pearson Education, Inc., All Rights Reserved

# Readers Theater/Read Aloud

**Directions:** Copy the rubric for individuals or groups. Rank individuals or groups for each skill.

| | 4 Excellent | 3 Good | 2 Satisfactory | 1 Needs Improvement |
|---|---|---|---|---|
| **BEFORE READING:** Research and practice part. | • Clearly demonstrates understanding of the organization and basic features of print.<br>• Plans own part and practices reading aloud with correct projection and diction.<br>• Consistently uses context to confirm or self-correct word recognition and understanding, rereading as necessary. (Grades 1–2)<br>• Consistently applies grade-level phonics and word analysis skills in decoding words. | • Demonstrates understanding of the organization and basic features of print.<br>• Plans part with some assistance and practices reading aloud with mostly correct projection and diction.<br>• Usually uses context to confirm or self-correct word recognition and understanding. (Grades 1–2)<br>• Usually applies grade-level phonics and word analysis skills in decoding words. | • Attempts to understand the organization and basic features of print.<br>• Attempts to plan own part and practices reading aloud with sometimes incorrect projection and diction.<br>• Occasionally uses context to confirm or self-correct word recognition and understanding. (Grades 1–2)<br>• Sometimes applies grade-level phonics and word analysis skills in decoding words. | • Does not understand the organization and basic features of print.<br>• Does not plan own part or practice reading aloud.<br>• Rarely if ever uses context to confirm or self-correct word recognition or understanding. (Grades 1–2)<br>• Rarely if ever applies grade-level phonics and word analysis skills in decoding words. |
| **WHILE READING ALOUD OR PERFORMING:** Communicate meaning with clear use of language and enthusiastic delivery. | • Consistently reads text with clear purpose and understanding, speaking clearly at an understandable pace.<br>• Consistently reads prose orally with accuracy, appropriate rate, and expression on successive readings to support comprehension (Grades 1–2 only).<br>• Understands the movement in front of a group; consistently maintains appropriate eye contact. | • Generally reads text with clear purpose and understanding, usually speaking clearly at an understandable pace.<br>• Generally reads prose orally with accuracy, appropriate rate, and expression on successive readings to support comprehension. (Grades 1–2)<br>• Usually understands the movement in front of a group; usually maintains appropriate eye contact. | • Attempts to read text with purpose and understanding, but sometimes does not speak clearly or at an understandable pace.<br>• Reads prose orally but there are a few errors in accuracy, rate, and/or expression, even on successive readings. (Grades 1–2)<br>• Sometimes understands the movement in front of a group; attempts to maintain appropriate eye contact. | • Does not read text with clear purpose or understanding.<br>• Does not read prose orally with accuracy, appropriate rate, or expression, even on successive readings. (Grades 1–2)<br>• Does not understand the movement in front of a group or maintain eye contact. |
| **AFTER READING:** Ask and answer questions about a reading of a text. | • Consistently asks and answers questions to clarify something that is not understood.<br>• Consistently builds on others' talk in conversations by responding to comments. (Grades 1–2) | • Often asks and answers questions to clarify something that is not understood.<br>• Often builds on others' talk in conversations by responding to comments. (Grades 1–2) | • Attempts to ask and answer questions to clarify something that is not understood.<br>• Attempts to build on others' talk in conversations by responding to comments. (Grades 1–2) | • Rarely if ever asks or answers questions to clarify something that is not understood.<br>• Rarely if ever builds on others' talk in conversations by responding to comments. (Grades 1–2) |

© Pearson Education, Inc., All Rights Reserved

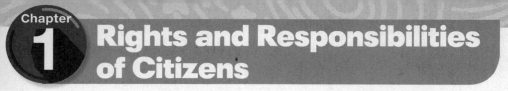

## Chapter 1

# Rights and Responsibilities of Citizens

## Objectives

- Explain the word *respect* as it pertains to a school community.
- Create classroom rules to make sure everyone is respected.
- Vote on the final set of rules through a shared discussion.

| **Quest** Shared Discussion: Who Needs Rules? | | | | |
|---|---|---|---|---|
| | **Description** | **Duration** | **Materials** | **Participants** |
| **STEP 1**<br>Set the Stage | Read a blackline master as an introduction to the project. | 15 minutes | **Blackline Master:** Quest Kick Off | Whole Class |
| **STEP 2**<br>Launch the Activities | Watch a video with background information. | 5 minutes | **Video:** How do people best cooperate?<br>**Leveled Readers:** Being a Good Citizen; The Importance of Rules; Rights and Responsibilities of Citizens | Whole Class |
| **Activity 1**<br>Respect | Read aloud a book and discuss respect. | 25 minutes | **Student Activity Mat:** 4A Let's Talk/How Many?<br>**Thinking Like a Citizen book:** *Why Can't I Say That?* | Whole Class |
| **Activity 2**<br>Class Rules | Create and discuss class rules. | 30 minutes | Chart paper | Small Groups |
| **Activity 3**<br>Shared Discussion | Prepare for a shared discussion. | 20 minutes | **Blackline Master:** Thinking About Rules | Individuals |
| **Activity 4**<br>Class Vote | Vote to select five rules for the classroom. | 25 minutes | Copies of suggested class rules, green crayon | Individuals |
| **STEP 3** ELL<br>Complete the Quest Shared Discussion | Facilitate a class discussion about rules and respect. | 30 minutes | **Blackline Master:** Thinking About Rules<br>**Student Activity Mat:** 4A Let's Talk/How Many? | Whole Class |
| Answer the **Compelling Question** | Discuss the compelling question. | 15 minutes | | Whole Class |

© Pearson Education, Inc., All Rights Reserved

## Quick Activities

| | Description | Duration | Materials | Participants |
|---|---|---|---|---|
| **Is It Fair?** | Decide if various scenarios are fair or unfair. | 15 minutes | **Blackline Master:** Fair or Unfair? | Individuals |
| **Good Sport** ELL | Create a word web describing the characteristics of a "good sport". | 20 minutes | Web organizers | Individuals |
| **Representative Democracy** | Discuss the differences between a representative democracy and a direct democracy. | 30 minutes | **Blackline Master:** Forms of Democracy | Small Groups |
| **Problem Solvers** | Discuss and form a solution to solve a hypothetical problem. | 20 minutes | | Small Groups |
| **Read Aloud:** The Monkey and the Crocodile | Listen to a retelling and act out an alternative ending. | 30 minutes | **Blackline Master:** The Monkey and the Crocodile | Whole Class |

© Pearson Education, Inc., All Rights Reserved

# Shared Discussion: Who Needs Rules?

 **How do rules make us more respectful?**

Welcome to Quest 1, Who Needs Rules? In this Quest, children will create classroom rules and vote to accept them. By identifying the importance of respect and rules, they will gain hands-on insight to discuss the compelling question at the end of this inquiry.

## Objectives

- Explain the word *respect* as it pertains to a school community.
- Create classroom rules to make sure everyone is respected.
- Vote on the final set of rules through a shared discussion.

## STEP 1  Set the Stage    ⏱ 15 minutes

Begin the Quest by distributing the blackline master **Quest Kick Off.** It will bring the world of the Quest to life, introducing a story to interest children and a mission to motivate them.

### Story

Three classmates need to work together to take care of the class pet. They all want to feed the class pet, but nobody wants to clean the cage. They begin to argue over who should be the one to feed him. Then one classmate calls the others mean names and upsets them.

The teacher hears them. She calls them together and tells them they need to come up with rules on how to work together. In order to keep the responsibility of taking care of the class pet, they need to show respect and follow rules.

### Mission

Work with your class to form a set of rules to create a respectful classroom.

© Pearson Education, Inc., All Rights Reserved

## STEP 2 Launch the Activities

The following four activities will help children prepare for their shared discussion by creating a set of classroom rules to foster respect. Note that all four can be done independently of the larger Quest. Begin by showing the video *How do people best cooperate?*, which will give children the content background they need to complete the activities. You may also assign the appropriate Leveled Reader for the chapter.

 **Respect** (25) **minutes**

**Materials:** Student Activity Mat 4A Let's Talk/How Many?, Thinking Like a Citizen book, *Why Can't I Say That?*

Ask children if they know what the word *respect* means. Have children write down their thoughts and ideas of what respect is and examples of showing respect on Student Activity Mat 4A **Let's Talk/How Many?**. Instruct children to listen to the story in the Thinking Like a Citizen book *Why Can't I Say That?* and think about respect. Read aloud the book.

Explain the word *respect* to children. Give examples of how to respect others, their feelings, and their property. Explain the importance of self-respect.

Then lead the children in a discussion about bullying. Suggested talking points: "Bullying is when someone is acting mean or hurtful to another person over and over again. Bullies try to hurt people and make them feel sad. Sometimes people disagree and that is OK. People can disagree or argue with one another once in a while. But if a person is being hurtful to another person over and over, then that is bullying."

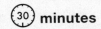 **Class Rules** (30) **minutes**

**Materials:** Chart paper

Explain that rules are necessary to make sure everyone is respectful. Remind children that in a school, it is important to show respect to the teacher, classmates, and the property of the school and others.

Divide the class into small groups. Instruct each group to think of rules that will make sure everyone feels respected. Guide groups to write rules that reflect the values of fair play and being a good sport and that respect the rights and opinions of others. Bring the class together and write the rules from each group on chart paper.

© Pearson Education, Inc., All Rights Reserved

## Activity 3   Shared Discussion    minutes

**Materials:** Blackline Master, *Thinking About Rules*

Distribute the blackline master **Thinking About Rules,** which asks children to support and explain their rules.

Explain how to have a discussion (use the Shared Discussion rubric). Have children focus on the importance of working together and how to listen and respond to what has been said.

Read sentence starters on the blackline master aloud, and give children time to write their responses. They will use these responses during the shared discussion.

## Activity 4   Class Vote    minutes

**Materials:** Chart Paper with suggested class rules (from Activity 2),
typed sheet with suggested rules for each child,
green crayon

Congratulate the class on working together in creating respectful rules. Have everyone give their neighbor a high-five because they ALL created rules to foster respect. Tell the class that although all the rules are amazing, you will only be able to write five onto the Classroom Rules chart.

Inform the class that in a direct democracy people have a say in the rulemaking process. So everyone will be able to vote on the five rules for the class.

Instruct children on how to vote. Distribute a copy of the rules to each child, and read through each rule. Instruct children to get out a green crayon. Tell them to circle the five rules they want for the class. Read each rule again, pausing for children to vote by circling the rule. Remind children they can only vote on five rules (circulate to monitor). Collect and count votes.

Before revealing the five rules, remind children that all of the rules were exceptional and that this isn't about winning—it is about having a respectful classroom. Reveal the five classroom rules.

© Pearson Education, Inc., All Rights Reserved

## Part 1 Shared Discussion ⏱ 30 minutes

**Materials:** Blackline Master Thinking About Rules, Student Activity Mat
4A Let's Talk/How Many?

Engage children in a discussion about the rules shared by each small group. Refer back to the story and mission. Guide children to explain how their rules will create a respectful classroom. Children can use their answers from the blackline master **Thinking About Rules** to explain and discuss their rules. Guide the discussion by asking: Who is responsible for enforcing the rules? What are the consequences if these rules are broken? Encourage children to use Student Activity Mat 4A **Let's Talk/How Many?** during their discussions.

Encourage children to discuss their understanding of respect for rules. Ask: What is the purpose of having rules? What would happen if we didn't have rules?

····················································································

### ⓔ Support for English Language Learners

**Speaking:** Have children practice elaborating on topics during a conversation. Point out that children should ask and answer questions to keep a discussion going.

**Entering:** Work with children to come up with *yes/no* questions they can ask about a class pet and how to be fair. As an example, ask: *Is it fair if only one person gets to pet the class pet?*

**Emerging:** Divide children into pairs. Have children think of three questions about class pets and how to be fair. Have children work together to answer each question.

**Developing:** Divide children into pairs. Have children think of two questions to ask their partner about the topic of class pets and how to be fair. Instruct the partners to ask and answer the questions following turn-taking rules.

**Expanding:** Divide children into pairs. Have children think of one question to ask their partner about the topic of class pets and how to be fair. Then have partners build off of the conversation by asking another question based on the given responses. Instruct the partners to ask and answer the questions following turn-taking rules.

**Bridging:** Have children form groups of three. Tell groups to discuss the topic of a class pet and how to be fair.

## Part 2 Answer the Compelling Question ⏱ 15 minutes

After children participate in a shared discussion, encourage them to reflect on what they learned. As a class, discuss the compelling question for this Quest, "How do rules make us more respectful?"

Children should use what they learned to answer the compelling question.

© Pearson Education, Inc., All Rights Reserved

# Who Needs Rules?

Three classmates need to work together to take care of the class pet. They all want to feed the class pet, but nobody wants to clean the cage. They begin to argue over who should be the one to feed him. Then one classmate calls the others mean names and upsets them.

> Your Mission: Work as a class to write rules for a respectful classroom.

The teacher hears them. She calls them together and tells them they need to come up with rules on how to work together. In order to keep the responsibility of taking care of the class pet, they need to show respect and follow rules.

© Pearson Education, Inc. All Rights Reserved

# To prepare for a shared discussion, work with the class to do the following:

**Activity 1** **Respect:** Listen to the read aloud, and explain the word *respect*.

**Activity 2** **Class Rules:** Create a set of class rules to show respect.

**Activity 3** **Shared Discussion:** Prepare for a shared discussion by recording responses about your rules.

**Activity 4** **Class Vote:** Vote to determine five classroom rules.

## Complete Your Quest

Discuss the rules shared by each small group and the importance of rules to have a respectful classroom.

© Pearson Education, Inc., All Rights Reserved

## Thinking About Rules

Complete the sentences.

We chose our rules because _____

_____

_____.

If a class rule is broken, then _____

_____

_____.

_____ is responsible for enforcing the rules.

Rules are important because _____

_____

_____.

© Pearson Education, Inc., All Rights Reserved

# Quick Activities

## Is It Fair?
**Individuals** (15) **minutes**

**Materials:** Blackline Master Fair or Unfair?

Distribute the blackline master **Fair or Unfair?,** which asks children to identify each action as fair or unfair.

Extend the activity by having children explain why they think each statement is fair or unfair.

## Good Sport
**Individuals** (20) **minutes**

**Materials:** Web organizer

Write the words *good sport* in the center of the web organizer before copying it for children. Explain what a "good sport" is to children by providing examples.

After discussing what a good sport is, instruct children to create a web. They can write descriptive words in the web, draw pictures in the web, or find pictures from magazines that describe what a good sport is.

© Pearson Education, Inc., All Rights Reserved

# Support for English Language Learners

**Speaking:** Children need to practice describing and understanding language choices. Children will evaluate the idea of being a "good sport" by thinking about and applying specific language choices.

**Entering:** Divide children into pairs to act out the following scenario:
*Classmate A: Did you hear the joke the teachers played on Principal Steve?*
*Classmate B: They told him to dress up for a costume party.*
*Classmate A: But there was no party. So only he wore a costume.*
*Classmate B: He just laughed. He is a good sport.*
Then have children discuss what a "good sport" is.

**Emerging:** Divide children into pairs. Discuss what being a "good sport" means. Have them act out a scenario that shows someone acting as a good sport. Children may need ideas such as the following: one soccer team is winning and being nice to the opposing team, or each child is making sure that everyone has the same amount of turns in using a jump-rope.

**Developing:** Divide children into pairs. Have children discuss what being a "good sport" means. Have them act out a scenario that shows someone acting as a good sport.

**Expanding:** Divide children into pairs. Have children discuss what being a "good sport" means. In small groups, have pairs act out a scenario that shows someone being a good sport. Have other group members determine who is being a good sport and how.

**Bridging:** Divide children into pairs. Have children come up with two different scenarios where they could use the phrase *good sport* in a conversation. Ask them to share their scenarios with another pair and discuss what being a "good sport" means.

# Representative Democracy

Small Groups  minutes

**Materials:** Blackline Master Forms of Democracy

Remind children of the direct democratic voting process they used to vote for the class rules. Inform children that there is another type of democracy: representative. Explain the term *representative democracy*.

Model a representative democracy by asking each table group to select a leader. Vote on the class rules again, but only count the votes of the table leaders. Point out the advantages and disadvantages of both voting models. Engage children in a discussion to understand citizenship and government.

Ask children to decide which form of democracy they prefer and group them based on their answer. Distribute the blackline master **Forms of Democracy.** Engage each group in a shared writing experience using the blackline master for guidance.

© Pearson Education, Inc., All Rights Reserved

## Problem Solvers

Small Groups 20 minutes

Teach or review the steps of problem-solving with children.

1. Identify the problem.
2. Gather information about it.
3. List ways to solve it.
4. Ask yourself: "Which way will work best?"
5. Choose a way and solve the problem.
6. Think about how well your plan worked.

Divide children into small groups. Assign each group one of the following dilemmas, and instruct them to discuss the problem and develop a possible solution.

- There aren't enough glue sticks for each group. What do you do?

- Two people in your group want to make a poster, but you want to make a diorama. What do you do?

- Your group must complete five tasks in order to finish a poster, but there are only three group members. What do you do?

- Your group chose you as their leader, but you don't want to be the leader. What do you do?

If time permits, children can act out their dilemma and solution as a way of presenting it to the whole class.

## Read Aloud

Whole Class 30 minutes

**Materials:** Blackline Master The Monkey and the Crocodile

Distribute the blackline master **The Monkey and the Crocodile.** Have children listen to the retelling of the story. Then have children discuss the trait of honesty as it pertains to the story.

Encourage children to read a paragraph from the story after hearing it read aloud. Have children read in pairs or do a choral reading.

After the story and discussion, group children and ask them to act out the story with a different ending.

© Pearson Education, Inc., All Rights Reserved

# Fair or Unfair?

Circle the correct response.

**1.** Someone takes an extra turn during a game.

Fair          Unfair

**2.** Someone shares the only ball with someone else.

Fair          Unfair

**3.** Someone cuts in front of someone else waiting in line.

Fair          Unfair

© Pearson Education, Inc. All Rights Reserved

## Forms of Democracy

Complete the sentences.

I think the _____

_____

democracy has the most advantages because

_____

_____. I prefer to

_____

vote using _____ democracy

because _____.

It is important to have everyone vote because

_____.

© Pearson Education, Inc., All Rights Reserved

Once upon a time, a monkey lived in a tree on the side of a river. Monkey was always happy even though he was alone. The tree gave him sweet fruit to eat, shade from the hot sun, and protection from the rain.

One day a crocodile climbed onto the side of the river to rest under Monkey's tree. "Hello," called friendly Monkey. "Let me offer you some of my sweet fruit."

Monkey threw down sweet fruit to Crocodile day after day. Crocodile would come back to enjoy Monkey's sweet fruit and their friendly chats.

One day, Crocodile invited Monkey to have dinner at his house on the other side of the river. "I should have invited you sooner," Crocodile said.

© Pearson Education, Inc., All Rights Reserved

"I would love to come, but I can not swim. How can I cross the river?" Monkey said.

"I will give you a ride on my back," Crocodile replied.

So Monkey climbed onto Crocodile's back, and they set off down the river.

Monkey asked, "May I ask what is for dinner?"

Crocodile felt safe telling Monkey the truth since it was too late for Monkey to escape. "You are for dinner, my sweet friend."

Monkey was scared. He needed to think fast.

"Oh no," said Monkey. "My sweetest part is my heart, and I left it back in my tree. Take me back and you can have it," Monkey exclaimed.

Crocodile turned and swam back to Monkey's tree. Once they were on the

© Pearson Education, Inc., All Rights Reserved

riverbank, Monkey jumped off and climbed into his tree.

"Crocodile, I will not be coming for dinner tonight or any night," Monkey declared.

Crocodile was very angry and ashamed that he fell for Monkey's lie. From that day on, monkeys have never trusted crocodiles.

© Pearson Education, Inc., All Rights Reserved

## Objectives

- Take a tour of the school and learn its physical environment.
- Create a flat map of the school.
- Use the flat map to create a diorama of the school and present it to the class.

| *Quest* Project-Based Learning: Get to Know My School | | | | |
|---|---|---|---|---|
| | **Description** | **Duration** | **Materials** | **Participants** |
| **STEP 1** Set the Stage | Read a blackline master as an introduction to the project. | 15 minutes | **Blackline Master:** Quest Kick Off | Whole Class |
| **STEP 2** Launch the Activities | Make relevant connections and build content background for the Quest. | 5 minutes | **Leveled Readers:** Getting Around School; Mapping the School; Getting to Know Our Environment | Whole Class |
| **Activity 1** Tour the School | Tour the school, take notes, and sketch a map. | 30 minutes | Tablet or dry erase board | Whole Class |
| **Activity 2** Create a Flat Map | Create a flat map of the school. | 45 minutes | **Blackline Master:** Places at School Butcher paper, crayons or markers, tape or glue | Small Groups |
| **Activity 3** Compare and Contrast Schools | Compare and contrast a layout of the school with another school. | 30 minutes | **Blackline Master:** Compare and Contrast Schools Completed flat map of school | Whole Class |
| **STEP 3** **ELL** Complete the Quest Create a Diorama | Create a diorama of the school using the completed flat map. | 60 minutes | **Blackline Master:** Prepare Your Presentation Shoe box or shipping box, scissors, construction paper, crayons or markers, tape or glue | Small Groups |
| Deliver a Presentation | Present a diorama to the class. | 45 minutes | **Blackline Master:** Prepare Your Presentation Completed diorama | Whole Class |
| Answer the **Compelling Question** | Discuss the compelling question. | 30 minutes | **Student Activity Mat:** 4A Let's Talk/How Many? | Whole Class |

© Pearson Education, Inc., All Rights Reserved

## Quick Activities

| | Description | Duration | Materials | Participants |
|---|---|---|---|---|
| **Neighborhood Map** | Create a map of a familiar neighborhood. | (30) minutes | Construction paper, crayons or markers | Individuals |
| **Visiting the Neighborhood** | Role-play visiting different places in the neighborhood. | (20) minutes | Props such as money, shopping bags, envelopes | Small Groups |
| **Study a Map** | Use cardinal directions to discuss locations on a map. | (20) minutes | **Blackline Master:** Study a Map | Small Groups |
| **Which Environment Am I?** ELL | Play a game to review environments and how they affect people. | (15) minutes | **Student Activity Mat:** 3A Graphic Organizer | Whole Class |
| **Readers Theater:** A Big Move | Perform a brief skit about a girl talking to her friend about moving from Georgia to Alaska. | (30) minutes | **Blackline Master:** A Big Move | Small Groups |

© Pearson Education, Inc., All Rights Reserved

# Project-Based Learning: Get to Know My School

**Compelling Question**

## How can we find our way?

Welcome to Quest 2, Get to Know My School. In this Quest, children will create a flat map based on a walking tour of the school. Children will use the flat map to construct a 3-D model (a diorama) of the school and school grounds. By studying the physical layout of the school, they will be prepared to discuss the compelling question at the end of this inquiry.

### Objectives

- Take a tour of the school and learn its physical environment.
- Create a flat map of the school.
- Use the flat map to create a diorama of the school and present it to the class.

### STEP 1 Set the Stage ⏱ 15 minutes

Begin the Quest by distributing the blackline master **Quest Kick Off.** It will bring the world of the Quest to life, introducing a story to interest children and a mission to motivate them.

---

### Story

This year, your class has several new children who don't know the layout of the school. The principal asked for volunteers to help your new classmates.

Let's help them by giving them a tour of the school. We will also draw a map, and then use the map to build a model of the school.

········································································

### Mission

You will need to show your new classmates the school and give them directions. You will build a diorama, or a model, of your school. By studying maps and exploring the school grounds, you can help the new children learn their way around your school.

---

© Pearson Education, Inc., All Rights Reserved

**Geography of the Community** 

Quest Teacher Material

## STEP 2 Launch the Activities

The following three activities will help children prepare for their project-based learning by touring the school, creating a flat map of the school, and constructing a diorama. Note that all three can be done independently of the larger Quest.

As you begin, give children an opportunity to build content background as a launch into the following activities. You may wish to assign the appropriate Leveled Readers for this chapter. Then ask children what they know about maps and how they relate to the school. Organize children into small groups that will remain consistent throughout the activities.

---

### Activity 1 Tour the School  minutes

**Materials:** Tablet or dry erase board

Explain to children that you will take them on a walking tour of the school and school grounds. On the tour, provide directions for the children, such as "We are turning left," and "We are turning right." As you walk, explicitly point out the different rooms in the school, such as the library, cafeteria, gym, their classroom, and so on. In addition, point out any ramps and other things that make the school accessible to children with disabilities (for example: buttons to automatically open doors, low-drinking water fountains).

At each stop on the school tour, use a tablet or dry erase board to map out the school. Show children the map and discuss. Be sure to point to the addition you made to the map and name it. Have children create their own sketch of the school and school grounds on a sheet of paper. This may be done during the walking tour, or after. Then, discuss the physical environment of the school and school grounds together.

---

### Activity 2 Create a Flat Map  minutes

**Materials:** Blackline Master Places at School, butcher paper, crayons or markers, tape or glue

Explain to children that they will use their sketches of the school and school grounds created in the previous activity to create a flat map of their school.

Have each group use butcher paper to create a flat map of their school based on their sketches. Tell them to include the different locations they sketched, such as the library, cafeteria, gym, and their classroom.

Distribute the blackline master **Places at School** to each group. Explain to children that they will color and cut out the images from the blackline master. Have groups decide who will color each image. Then, have groups use tape or glue to add the images onto the butcher paper. Encourage groups to draw additional school-related images on the butcher paper that are not on the blackline master.

© Pearson Education, Inc., All Rights Reserved

## Activity 3 | Compare and Contrast Schools ⏰30 minutes

**Materials:** Blackline Master Compare and Contrast Schools,
Completed flat map of school (from Activity 2)

Explain to children that they will compare and contrast the layout of their flat maps with the layout of another school.

Distribute the blackline master **Compare and Contrast Schools,** which shows the layout of a fictional school. With children, discuss the different locations on the blackline master school. Then, ask children how they could go from one area of the blackline master school to another area. Help children use spatial words when discussing the location of the different places. Then, have children compare and contrast the blackline master school with their flat maps. Prompt a discussion by asking, "How are the two schools similar? How are they different?"

If there are children who have attended different schools, ask them to explain how the layout of their old school was similar and different than the school they are currently attending.

© Pearson Education, Inc., All Rights Reserved

**Part 1** Create a Diorama (60) minutes

**Materials:** Blackline Master Prepare Your Presentation, shoe box or shipping box, scissors, construction paper, crayons or markers, tape or glue, cardboard

After children have completed the activities, have them work in groups and use their flat maps to create a diorama (3-D model) of their school and school grounds. Work with children to label the different locations of the school on the diorama. When children are finished, have them compare the flat map with the diorama. Discuss the type of information the flat map provides as compared to the model.

Explain to children that they will work in teams to prepare their presentations of the dioramas. Distribute the blackline master **Prepare Your Presentation** for children to use as sentence starters for their presentations. Encourage children to write down their answers and to take turns presenting in their group.

**ELL Support for English Language Learners**

*Speaking:* Remind children to use the proper vocabulary as they prepare their presentations. The activities here will help them practice their skill.

**Entering:** Write the vocabulary used to describe the different locations of the school on index cards. As you display an index card and read the vocabulary word aloud, point to the corresponding location on their diorama. Have children repeat the vocabulary word after you. Give children one phrase they can use in their presentations. Be sure to include at least one vocabulary word.

**Emerging:** Write the vocabulary used to describe the different locations of the school on index cards. Display an index card and read the vocabulary word aloud. Have children repeat the vocabulary word after you. Then have children write down two of the vocabulary words they will use in their presentations.

**Developing:** Write the vocabulary used to describe the different locations of the school on index cards. Display an index card and read the vocabulary word aloud. Have children repeat the vocabulary word after you, and then have them point to the corresponding location on their diorama. Then have children write down three vocabulary words they will use in their presentations.

**Expanding:** Write the vocabulary used to describe the different locations of the school on index cards. Display an index card and read the vocabulary word aloud. Have children repeat the vocabulary word and point to the corresponding location on their diorama. Then have children write down three or four vocabulary words they will use in their presentations. In pairs, have children take turns practicing the vocabulary and pointing to the corresponding location on their diorama.

**Bridging:** Write the vocabulary used to describe the different locations of the school on index cards. Then point to different locations on the diorama, and have children find the index card with the vocabulary word that corresponds to the location. Then have children write down four vocabulary words they will use in their presentations.

© Pearson Education, Inc., All Rights Reserved

**Part 2** **Deliver a Presentation** (45) minutes

**Materials:** Completed Blackline Master Prepare Your Presentation, completed dioramas

Have children present their dioramas to the class using the completed blackline master **Prepare Your Presentation**.

As groups present their group diorama to the class, make sure each group member contributes at least one idea or sentence. At the end of each presentation, allow time for audience members to ask questions about the diorama.

**Part 3** **Answer the Compelling Question** (30) minutes

**Materials:** Student Activity Mat 4A Let's Talk/How Many?

After all groups have finished presenting their dioramas, encourage them to reflect on what they learned. As a class, discuss the compelling question for this Quest: "How can we find our way?"

Children have learned how to create a flat map and diorama of their school and school grounds. Encourage children to think about how they would map other locations, such as their home or neighborhood. They should use what they learned to answer the compelling question. Children may want to record the ideas that are discussed on Student Activity Mat 4A **Let's Talk/How Many?**

© Pearson Education, Inc., All Rights Reserved

Name _____ Date _____

# Get to Know My School

This year, your class has many new children. The new children need help finding their way around their new school. The principal asked for volunteers to help your new classmates.

Let's help them by giving them a tour of the school. We will also draw a map, and then use the map to build a model of the school.

**Your Mission:**
You will need to show your new classmates the school and give them directions. You will build a diorama, or a model, of your school. By studying maps and exploring the school grounds, you can help the new children learn their way around your school.

© Pearson Education, Inc., All Rights Reserved

**To create a diorama of your school, do the following:**

**Activity 1** **Tour the School:** Take a tour of your school.

**Activity 2** **Create a Flat Map:** Make a map of your school.

**Activity 3** **Compare and Contrast Schools:** Talk about how your school is similar and different from other schools.

## Complete Your Quest

Create a diorama of your school, and then present your diorama to the class.

© Pearson Education, Inc., All Rights Reserved

Name _____ Date _____

# Places at School

Color the pictures. Then cut and paste the pictures on your flat map.

| | | |
|---|---|---|
| **Computer Lab** | **Gym** | **Principal's Office** |
|  |  |  |
| **Cafeteria** | **Library** | **Restroom** |
| 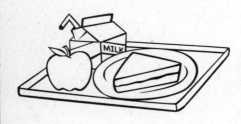 |  |  |
| **Playground** | **Classroom** | |
|  |  | |

© Pearson Education, Inc., All Rights Reserved

Name _____ Date _____

## Compare and Contrast Schools

Compare and contrast your school with the school below. How are they alike? How are they different?

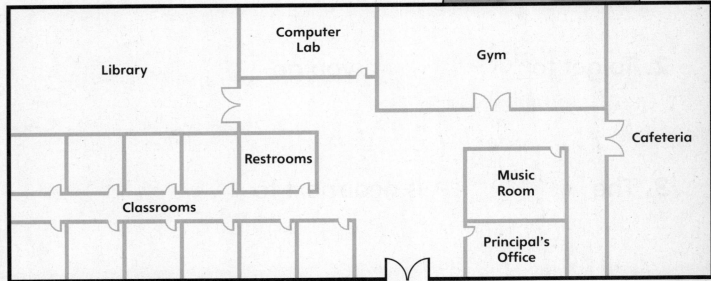

© Pearson Education, Inc., All Rights Reserved

 **Findings**

# Prepare Your Presentation

You have created a diorama of your school. Now it's time to present your diorama to the class. Use the sentences below to help you during your presentation.

**1.** In my school, there is/are _____.

**2.** To get to _____, you go _____.

**3.** The _____ is near/next to _____.

**4.** My favorite area in the school is _____.

© Pearson Education, Inc. All Rights Reserved

# Quick Activities

## Neighborhood Map

Individuals  30 minutes

**Materials:** Construction paper, crayons or markers

Have children create a map of their neighborhood or another neighborhood with which they are familiar. Ask children to label places on the neighborhood map. Remind children to add a legend and a compass rose. Provide support as needed.

Then, have children discuss what their neighborhood is like with a partner. Ask them to share where they live, shop, visit, play, and eat.

## Visiting the Neighborhood

Small Groups 20 minutes

**Materials:** Props such as money, shopping bags, envelopes

Organize children into two groups. Assign one group of children as people who work in the neighborhood, such as at the supermarket, bank, post office, or other places with which children are familiar. Have children space themselves around the classroom.

Assign the second group to be people running errands in the neighborhood. Assign them different tasks, such as shopping for groceries, taking out money, or mailing a letter, that would bring them into contact with the first group.

Ask children to role-play and interact with each other. If time permits, have groups switch roles. When children are finished, have them discuss what it is like to live in a neighborhood and community.

© Pearson Education, Inc., All Rights Reserved

## Study a Map

**Materials:** Blackline Master Study a Map

Organize children into small groups. Distribute blackline master **Study a Map**, which shows a neighborhood.

Display blackline master **Study a Map** and point out the compass rose. Explain that cardinal directions tell the direction of north, south, east, and west. Use the locations on the map to explain how to use the cardinal directions, such as how the supermarket is south of the post office. Provide several examples. Then, ask small groups to come up with their own directions using examples from the map.

Then, place blackline master **Study a Map** upright. Explain that although the map is in a different position, the places on the map still have the same relationship with one another. For example, the supermarket is still north of the post office.

## Which Environment Am I?

Whole Class 15 minutes

**Materials:** Student Activity Mat 3A Graphic Organizer

Spend time discussing different environments. Compare clothing, food, shelter, transportation, and recreational activities of each environment. Discuss how environments and people are connected.

Then, play a game to review environments and environmental effects. Play "Which Environmental Am I?" Provide clues to the environment you are describing and have children guess the environment. For example, say, *"I am dry. A cactus can grow here. You better pack your hat and sunglasses when you come and visit me! A lot of homes here are made of clay and brick. Which environment am I?"*

Have children use the Student Activity Mat 3A **Graphic Organizer** to record their clues.

© Pearson Education, Inc., All Rights Reserved

##  Support for English Language Learners

**Speaking:** Some English learners may need assistance in determining how an environment and people are connected.

Remind children to refer back to the discussion at the beginning of the exercise. Tell them to think of reasons how and why the environment and people are connected.

**Entering:** In small groups, play the game "Which Environment Am I?" Pause after each description to ask children *yes/no* questions about the environment you are describing. For example, ask: *Would you wear a winter jacket in this environment?*

**Emerging:** In small groups, play the game "Which Environment Am I?" Pause after each description to ask children *yes/no* questions about the environment you are describing. For example, ask: *Would you wear a winter jacket in this environment?* After children respond with *yes* or *no*, have them provide one reason why. Encourage children to use the word *because* in their oral responses. Continue pausing to ask *yes/no* questions so that students can support their opinions and guess the environment correctly.

**Developing:** In pairs, play the game "Which Environment Am I?" Pause after each description to ask children *yes/no* questions about the environment you are describing. For example, ask: *Would you wear a winter jacket in this environment?* After children respond with *yes* or *no*, have them provide one reason why. Encourage children to use the word *because* in their oral responses. Continue pausing to ask *yes/no* questions so that students can support their opinions and guess the environment correctly. Then have pairs practice playing the game with each other. Remind children to support their opinions.

**Expanding:** Play the game "Which Environment Am I?" When children guess, have them provide one supporting reason why they made the guess. Encourage children to use the word *because* in their oral responses.

**Bridging:** Pair children and have them play the game "Which Environment Am I?" with each other. Remind children to support their opinions.

© Pearson Education, Inc., All Rights Reserved

## Study a Map

Look at the different places on the map. Find the N, S, E, and W on the compass rose.

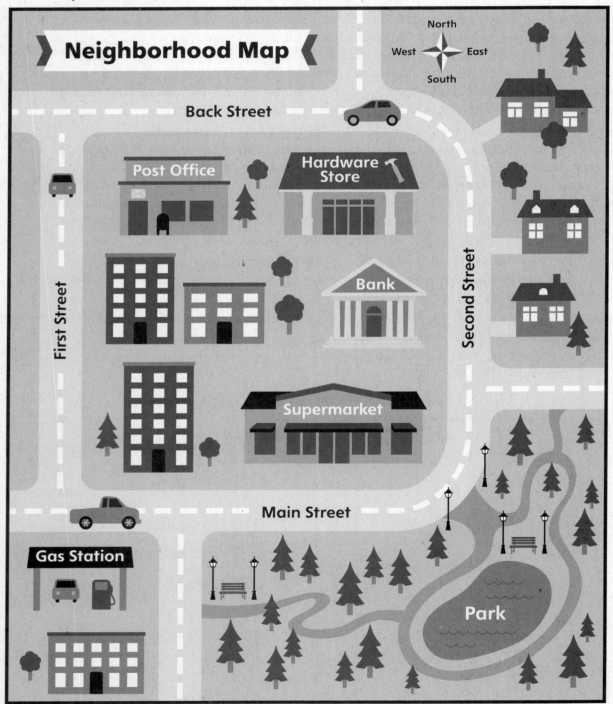

**32**

© Pearson Education, Inc. All Rights Reserved

## Readers Theater
## A Big Move

A story about a girl named Sarah who talks to her friend, Mina, about moving to Alaska.

### The Parts

*3 players:*

- **Sarah**, age 7, is moving to Alaska
- **Mina**, age 7, is Sarah's friend
- **Narrator**

*Director's Notes:*

*Set the stage as needed.*
*Sarah has a map of North America.*

**Narrator:** This is Sarah. Sarah is in first grade at a school just like yours. Sarah and her family are moving.

**Sarah:** We are moving to Alaska!
*begins packing her suitcase,*

© Pearson Education, Inc., All Rights Reserved

*Mina enters*

**Narrator:** Meet Mina. Mina is also in first grade. Mina is visiting Sarah before she moves.

**Mina:**
*sad, but then excited*

I am sad you are moving. But Alaska sounds really cool.

**Sarah:** It is! My dad says that Alaska is very different from Georgia.

**Mina:** How so?

**Sarah:**
*separates her summer clothes from her winter clothes*

It has lots of snow. Here in Georgia, we can wear sandals, it is mostly warm, and the sun shines.
In Alaska, people have to wear boots and heavy coats, and sometimes it is dark during the day. And, there are polar bears everywhere!

**Mina:** Polar bears! Really?

© Pearson Education, Inc., All Rights Reserved

**Sarah:**
*giggles*

Okay, so maybe the polar bear part is not true. But people do have to wear winter jackets and boots.

**Mina:**

How will you get around? Will your family drive a car?

**Sarah:**

Yes. Dad said we will also use a snowmobile to get from place to place. He also mentioned that dog mushing is a fun sport in Alaska.

**Mina:**

Mushing?! That is an interesting word. What is mushing?

**Sarah:**
*pretends to be in a sled, holding the reins*

That is when dogs pull you on a sled. That was the way people in Alaska used to get around. Now people do it for fun. I guess there is a big race or something. Did I tell you that Alaska has mountains?

**Mina:**

We have mountains in Georgia.

© Pearson Education, Inc., All Rights Reserved

**Sarah:** *looking up at the imagined height* The mountains in Alaska are bigger. One mountain peak is over 20,000 feet up in the air.

**Mina:** How are you getting there?

**Narrator:** Sarah shows Mina a map.

**Sarah:** *traces the route on the map with her finger* We are driving north to Canada. When we reach the northern part of Canada, we're heading west into Alaska.

**Mina:** Will you be close to a glacier?

**Sarah:** What's a glacier?

**Mina:** A glacier is a giant piece of ice. Some glaciers are as tall as a building. Some hikers climb glaciers!

**Sarah:** Maybe we can look at a glacier when you visit me!

**Narrator:** As Sarah and Mina made plans to visit each other, Sarah was really glad she talked to Mina about her move. She might be leaving Georgia, but she was not losing her friend.

© Pearson Education, Inc. All Rights Reserved

# 3 Symbols and Traditions of the United States

## Objectives

- Learn about a national or state holiday.
- Interview a family member about the holiday.
- Give an oral presentation about the holiday to the class.

## *Quest* Project-Based Learning: Our Holidays

| | Description | Duration | Materials | Participants |
|---|---|---|---|---|
| **STEP 1** Set the Stage | Read a blackline master as an introduction to the project. | 15 minutes | **Blackline Master:** Quest Kick Off | Whole Class |
| **STEP 2** Launch the Activities | Divide children into small groups. | 5 minutes | **Leveled Readers:** Learning About Holidays; Why Do We Celebrate?; The Background Behind Our Holidays | Small Groups |
| **Activity 1** Talk about the Holidays | Discuss and begin research on national and state holidays. | 30 minutes | **Blackline Master:** My Holiday | Small Groups |
| **Activity 2** Interview a Family Member | Interview a family member about a national or state holiday. | 30 minutes | **Blackline Master:** Interview Questions | Individuals |
| **Activity 3** Holiday Poster | Create a poster about a national or state holiday. | 30 minutes | Scissors, construction paper, tape, glue, markers, paint, magazines | Small Groups |
| **STEP 3** ELL Complete the Quest Writing a Presentation | Write their oral presentation. | 30 minutes | **Blackline Master:** Prepare Your Presentation | Small Groups |
| Deliver a Presentation | Give oral presentations about their holiday using poster. | 30 minutes | | Whole Class |
| Answer the Compelling **Question** | Discuss the compelling question. | 30 minutes | | Whole Class |

© Pearson Education, Inc., All Rights Reserved

| | Description | Duration | Materials | Participants |
|---|---|---|---|---|
| **Founding Fathers Flash Cards** | Research and write a paragraph about a Founding Father. | 15 minutes | Oversized index cards | Partners |
| **The American Flag** | Discuss the history of the American flag and then construct the American flag out of construction paper. | 20 minutes | **Blackline Master:** The American Flag Construction paper (red, white, and blue), scissors, tape, glue | Partners |
| **The Pledge of Allegiance** | "Rewrite" the Pledge of Allegiance by choosing the correct word. | 15 minutes | **Blackline Master:** The Pledge of Allegiance | Whole Class |
| **American Heroes** ELL | Take a quick poll of everyday heroes and write a short paragraph. | 30 minutes | **Student Activity Mat:** 3A Graphic Organizer **Student Activity Mat:** 4A Let's Talk/How Many? | Individuals, Whole Class |
| **Readers Theater:** The Declaration of Independence | Perform a brief skit about the writing and signing of the Declaration of Independence. | 15 minutes | **Blackline Master:** The Declaration of Independence | Small Groups, Whole Class |

© Pearson Education, Inc., All Rights Reserved

# Project-Based Learning: Our Holidays

 **Compelling Question** ## Why do we celebrate our holidays?

Welcome to Quest 3, Our Holidays. In this Quest, children will research a national or state holiday, interview a family member about the holiday, and then deliver a presentation about the holiday. By learning about different national and state holidays, they will be prepared to discuss the compelling question at the end of this inquiry.

## Objectives

- Learn about a national or state holiday.
- Interview a family member about the holiday.
- Give an oral presentation about the holiday to the class.

## STEP 1  Set the Stage  ⏱ 15 minutes

Begin the Quest by distributing the blackline master **Quest Kick Off.** It will bring the world of the Quest to life, introducing a story to interest children and a mission to motivate them.

### Story

Your school is having a culture showcase night. Children will present their research on holidays.

### Mission

Children have been given the task of telling the origin and significance of national and state holidays, why the holidays are important to our culture, and the many ways people celebrate them.

© Pearson Education, Inc., All Rights Reserved

## STEP 2 Launch the Activities

The following three activities will help children prepare for their presentation by helping them research their holiday and create a poster. Note that all three can be done independently of the larger Quest. You may wish to assign the appropriate Leveled Readers for the chapter.

### Activity 1  Talk about the Holidays  (30) minutes

**Materials:** Blackline Master My Holiday

Explain to children that they will research different national or state holidays. Begin by discussing some national or state holidays that they celebrate at school or at home.

Then divide the class into small groups. Assign a national or state holiday to each group. Some ideas for holidays include:

• Thanksgiving
• Independence Day
• Martin Luther King, Jr. Day
• Presidents' Day
• Memorial Day
• Labor Day
• Rosa Parks Day

Have groups gather information from provided resources to investigate the significance of the holidays. Tell children to gather information using the Library Media Center, as well as the following link:

http://wosu.pbslearningmedia.org/collection/holidays/

Distribute blackline master **My Holiday**, which contains questions that children should answer during their research. Have children write their information on the blackline master.

### Activity 2  Interview a Family Member  (30) minutes

**Materials:** Blackline Master Interview Questions

After groups have researched their holiday, explain to them that they will interview a family member about any family traditions they follow for that particular holiday.

Distribute blackline master **Interview Questions,** which contains a list of interview questions children can ask their family member. Have children write any additional interview questions they generate on their own on the blackline master.

Before children interview a family member, have them practice asking the interview questions to a classmate.

© Pearson Education, Inc., All Rights Reserved

**Activity 3** Holiday Poster ⏱ **30** minutes

**Materials:** Scissors, construction paper, tape, glue, markers, paint, magazines

Have groups work together to create a poster that represents their holiday. Groups should use art supplies and images from magazines or the Internet to decorate their posters.

In addition, tell children to include important information that they gather through research or during their interviews about their holiday.

# STEP 3 Complete the *Quest*

**Part 1** Writing a Presentation ⏱ **30** minutes

**Materials:** Blackline Master Prepare Your Presentation

After children have completed the activities above, have them work in groups to prepare their oral presentations. Distribute the blackline master **Prepare Your Presentation,** which contains sentence starters for children to use. Tell children to complete the sentences to use for their presentations. Once children have completed their blackline masters, have children practice their oral presentations with a partner or family member.

## ⓔ Support for English Language Learners

*Speaking:* Remind children to generate the proper vocabulary as they prepare their presentations. The activities here will help them practice their skill.

**Entering:** Write the children's holiday at the top of the sheet of paper. Then write three nouns that are associated with the holiday. Say each word aloud and have children repeat after you. Define any unfamiliar words. Then have children use the nouns in their presentations.

**Emerging:** Write the children's holiday at the top of the sheet of paper. Then write three nouns and three verbs that are associated with the holiday. Define any unfamiliar words. Then have children use the nouns and verbs in their presentations.

**Developing:** Write the children's holiday at the top of the sheet of paper. Then, with children, write one noun, one verb, and one adjective that are associated with the holiday. Define any unfamiliar words. Then have children use the noun, verb, and adjective in their presentations.

**Expanding:** Write the children's holiday at the top of the sheet of paper. Then, with children, write three nouns, three verbs, and three adjectives that are associated with the holiday. Define any unfamiliar words. Then have children use the nouns, verbs, and adjectives in their presentations.

**Bridging:** Write the children's holiday at the top of the sheet of paper. Then have children generate as many nouns, verbs, and adjectives as they can that are associated with the holiday. Then have children use the words in their presentations.

© Pearson Education, Inc., All Rights Reserved

## Part 2 Deliver a Presentation  minutes

Explain to children that they will have a cultural showcase night. They will talk about how and why people celebrate national and state holidays.

Have groups give their oral presentations about their holiday using the poster they created. For their presentation, have children answer the following questions:

- What is the holiday?
- What does this holiday celebrate?
- Why is this holiday important?
- How do you celebrate this holiday?
- How do you decorate for this holiday?
- Does your family have any traditions for this holiday? If so, what are they?

After each presentation, have children take turns using their listening skills to ask the presenters one clarifying question. Children will then answer the questions about their holiday.

## Part 3 Answer the Compelling Question 15 minutes

After groups have finished presenting information about their holidays, encourage them to reflect on what they learned. As a class, discuss the compelling question for this Quest, "Why do we celebrate our holidays?"

Children have learned how to research information, prepare for and conduct an interview, and prepare a presentation. Encourage children to think about other holidays that they celebrate and would like to research. They should use what they learned to answer the compelling question.

© Pearson Education, Inc., All Rights Reserved

Name _____     Date _____

# OUR HOLIDAYS

Your school is having a culture showcase night! Your class must tell how and why people celebrate national and state holidays. Learn more about the holidays by researching and interviewing family members. You will also create a poster that tells about the holiday. Finally, you will present your findings at the culture showcase night!

Your Mission:
Get ready for culture showcase night at school! Prepare for your presentation about how and why people celebrate your chosen national and state holidays.

© Pearson Education, Inc., All Rights Reserved

# To prepare and deliver your presentation, do the following:

**Activity 1** **Talk about the Holidays:** Learn more about national and state holidays.

**Activity 2** **Interview a Family Member:** Talk to a family member about a holiday.

**Activity 3** **Holiday Poster:** Create a poster that tells about your holiday.

## Complete Your Quest

Give an oral presentation about your holiday and share your poster with the class.

© Pearson Education, Inc., All Rights Reserved

## My Holiday

Learn more about your chosen holiday by answering the questions.

Name of my holiday: _____

**1.** Why do we celebrate this holiday?

_____
_____
_____

**2.** Why is this holiday important?

_____
_____
_____

**3.** How do people decorate for this holiday?

_____
_____
_____

© Pearson Education, Inc., All Rights Reserved

**4.** Does your holiday celebrate a person? If so, what did this person do?

_____

_____

_____

© Pearson Education, Inc., All Rights Reserved

## Interview Questions

Ask a family member the following questions about your holiday.

**1.** What does the holiday celebrate?

_____

_____

**2.** Why is this holiday important?

_____

_____

_____

**3.** How do you celebrate this holiday?

_____

_____

_____

© Pearson Education, Inc., All Rights Reserved

**4.** How do you decorate for this holiday?

_____

_____

_____

**5.** Does your family have any traditions for this holiday? If so, what are they?

_____

_____

_____

© Pearson Education, Inc. All Rights Reserved

# Prepare Your Presentation

You have created a poster about your holiday. Now it is time to present your holiday to the class. Complete the sentences below to help you during your presentation.

**1.** My holiday is _____.

**2.** My holiday celebrates _____.

**3.** My holiday is important because _____

_____.

**4.** We celebrate this holiday by _____

_____.

**5.** My family's traditions include _____

_____.

© Pearson Education, Inc., All Rights Reserved

# Quick Activities

## Founding Fathers Flash Cards

Partners ⏱15 minutes

**Materials:** Oversized index cards

Organize children into pairs. Then assign each pair one of the following Founding Fathers: Thomas Jefferson, Benjamin Franklin, John Adams, John Hancock

Have children research and write a short paragraph about their Founding Fathers on an oversized index card. Children should include their founder's name, the state they represented, and two interesting facts. When they complete the paragraph, have children draw an illustration of their founder on the back of the card.

Provide the following sentence frames for children:

_____ is called a Founding Father. _____ is from the state of _____. One fact about him is _____. Another fact is _____.

For more information, visit the following website:

https://www.archives.gov/founding-docs/founding-fathers

## The American Flag

Partners ⏱20 minutes

**Materials:** Blackline Master The American Flag, construction paper (red, white, and blue), scissors, glue

Distribute blackline master **The American Flag** and read the information in the fun fact box aloud. As a class, discuss the history of the American flag and the history behind the number of stars and stripes on the flag.

In pairs, have children complete the American flag outline on the blackline master using construction paper. Have them cut 7 red and 6 white stripes and a blue rectangle. Tell children to glue the stripes and blue background in the correct areas of blackline master **The American Flag.** Finally, have children draw stars or use stickers on the blue field.

Note: It is not necessary for children to include all 50 stars on their flag.

© Pearson Education, Inc., All Rights Reserved

## The Pledge of Allegiance

**Whole Class** (15) **minutes**

**Materials:** Blackline Master The Pledge of Allegiance

Begin the activity by having the class recite the Pledge of Allegiance.

Distribute blackline master **The Pledge of Allegiance.** Explain to children that they will "rewrite" the Pledge of Allegiance by completing the poem with the words that best capture the meaning of some of its key words.

Read aloud each line of the original poem (below), pausing at each word in **bold.** Give children enough time to choose the word that best expresses the meaning of that key word. Continue the activity until children have circled all the answer choices.

Provide appropriate support each time you come to a key word. Use words in a sentence or provide synonyms to help children understand their meaning.

> I **pledge** allegiance to the Flag of the United States of America, and to the Republic for which it stands, one **Nation** under God, indivisible, with **liberty** and **justice** for all.

## American Heroes

**Individuals, Whole Class**  **minutes**

**Materials:** Student Activity Mat 4A Let's Talk/How Many?

Write the names of American heroes, such as George Washington, Rosa Parks, César Chávez, and Martin Luther King, Jr., on the board. Discuss with children the qualities that make these people heroes.

Have children circulate around the room for 10 minutes and ask two or three classmates about everyday heroes they know. They can name firefighters, parents, or people from school. Ask children to record their questions and their classmates answers on the Student Activity Mat 4A **Let's Talk/How Many?**

Finally, have children write a short paragraph about an American hero. Encourage children to write about one of the people their classmates named and why this person is an American hero. Provide support as needed. Collect the paragraphs and make a class book of American heroes.

© Pearson Education, Inc., All Rights Reserved

## ⓔ Support for English Language Learners

*Writing:* During this activity, children will write a paragraph about an American hero. Tell children that the words *first, next, then,* and *finally* are used to connect ideas together in sequential order. You may wish to provide Student Activity Mat 3A **Graphic Organizer** so students can draw examples labeled with various sequence words such as *first, next, then,* and *finally*.

Remind children to use sequential words to connect ideas as they write about an American hero.

**Entering:** Write the following example on the board: *First, I got out of bed. Next, I ate breakfast. Then, I put on my jacket. Finally, I walked to school.* As you read aloud the sentences, use gestures to pantomime the actions. Then explain how the first word in each sentence tells the order of events. Then help children use sequential words to connect ideas in their paragraph.

**Emerging:** Write the following example on the board: *First, I got out of bed. Next, I ate breakfast. Then, I put on my jacket. Finally, I walked to school.* Read aloud the sentences with children. Underline the sequential word in each sentence and explain how they tell the order of events. Then have children use sequential words to connect ideas in their paragraph.

**Developing:** Write the sequential words *first, next, then,* and *finally* on the board and explain their meanings. Then write the following example on the board: _____, *I got out of bed.* _____, *I ate breakfast.* _____, *I put on my jacket.* _____, *I walked to school.* Read aloud the sentences with children. Have them write the correct sequential word in each sentence. Then have children use sequential words to connect ideas in their paragraph.

**Expanding:** Write the sequential words *first, next, then,* and *finally* on the board and explain their meanings. In pairs, have children generate sentences using the sequential words in the proper sequence. After children have practiced using them, have children use sequential words to connect ideas in their paragraph.

**Bridging:** Write the sequential words *first, next, then,* and *finally* on the board. Have children explain their meanings. Then have children generate sentences using the sequential words in the proper sequence. Then have children use sequential words to connect ideas in their paragraph.

© Pearson Education, Inc., All Rights Reserved

# Readers Theater, The Declaration of Independence

**Whole Class, Small Groups** (15) **minutes**

**Materials:** Blackline Master The Declaration of Independence

Explain to children that in this Readers Theater they will act out a scene about the writing and signing of the Declaration of Independence.

Distribute the blackline master **The Declaration of Independence,** which contains the script for the Readers Theater. Point out the different roles, dialogue, and the director's notes. If necessary, explain to children that the dialogue is the conversation between two or more characters. The director's notes give information about the play that isn't in the dialogue.

Organize children into small groups and assign a role to each child. Allow groups time to read over the script and become familiar with the dialogue. Work with children as they read their parts aloud as practice. If necessary, provide support for any vocabulary children may be unfamiliar with.

Arrange the class in a semicircle facing an open area of the classroom. Then have groups perform for the class. Tell children they should read with accuracy, appropriate rate, and expression. Audience members should listen quietly and not interrupt the performers.

© Pearson Education, Inc., All Rights Reserved

Name _____ Date _____

# The American Flag

## Fun Fact

Betsy Ross made the first American flag. Today, it has 50 stars. There is one star for each of the 50 states in our country. The 13 stripes represent the 13 colonies that declared independence from England in 1776.

© Pearson Education, Inc., All Rights Reserved

# The Pledge of Allegiance

Circle the correct word that best completes the Pledge of Allegiance. Use the Pledge of Allegiance to help you figure out which word fits the best.

I (promise/take) allegiance to the flag of the United States of America, and to the Republic for which it stands, one (government/house), under God, indivisible with (freedom/loyalty) and (niceness/fairness) for all.

© Pearson Education, Inc., All Rights Reserved

# Readers Theater
# The Declaration of Independence

This is the story of how the Declaration of Independence was written and approved.

## The Parts

*Six players:*

- **Narrator**
- **Thomas Jefferson**, writer of the Declaration of Independence
- **John Adams**, helped in the Independence Movement
- **Benjamin Franklin**, helped edit the Declaration of Independence
- **Robert E. Livingston**, also helped
- **Roger Sherman**, helped, too

*Director's Notes:*

*The play is a fictional account about the writing and approval of the Declaration of Independence.*

© Pearson Education, Inc., All Rights Reserved

| | |
|---|---|
| **Narrator:** | The year is 1776. Representatives from the 13 colonies gather in Philadelphia. They decide to declare their independence from England. They need to tell the world they are free. Thomas Jefferson and John Adams try to decide who should write the Declaration: |
| **Jefferson:** *looking tired* | You write it. |
| **Adams:** *looking very determined* | No. |
| **Jefferson:** *looking even more tired* | Come on! Please? |
| **Adams:** *looking even more determined* | No. |
| **Jefferson:** *looking surprised* | Why not? |

© Pearson Education, Inc., All Rights Reserved

**Adams:**

*smiling at Jefferson*

Everyone likes you. And, you are a better writer than I am.

**Jefferson:**

*realizing what an important moment this is*

I will be proud to write our Declaration my friend.

**Narrator:**

Thomas Jefferson works for two weeks before bringing his draft for others to edit. Benjamin Franklin, Robert E. Livingston, and Roger Sherman help.

**Jefferson:**

*running to them with a document in his hand*

I am finished with my first draft!

**Franklin:**

Did you write about how all people are born with rights?

**Jefferson:**

I did!

**Livingston:**

What about that government should help all the people, and not just the rulers?

**Jefferson:**

*pointing to that part of the document*

That is in there.

© Pearson Education, Inc., All Rights Reserved

**Sherman:** Now it is time to edit it.

**Jefferson:** Ugh!

*goes from excited to tired once more*

**Narrator:** They go over each word of the draft for three days until it is just right.

**Franklin:** Take out that paragraph!

**Livingston:** Change that word!

**Sherman:** Rewrite that sentence!

**Jefferson:** Ugh!

**Narrator:** Finally, the Declaration of Independence is complete. On July 4, 1776, the representatives of the 13 colonies gather again and approve the finished document. A bell rings out from a nearby church to announce the news.

© Pearson Education, Inc., All Rights Reserved

## Chapter 4

# Life Today and Long Ago

## Objectives

- Compare and contrast topics, including school, work, transportation, clothing, games, and holidays, and determine how they have changed over time.

- Create a timeline about the topic.
- Write an informational/expository paragraph comparing and contrasting our lives today with those from the past.

### *Quest* Writing Using Sources: Blast From the Past

| | Description | Duration | Materials | Participants |
|---|---|---|---|---|
| **STEP 1** <br> Set the Stage | Read a blackline master as an introduction to the project. | 15 minutes | **Blackline Master:** Quest Kick Off | Whole Class |
| **STEP 2** <br> Launch the Activities | Divide children into small groups to ask questions and discuss the chapter topic. | 5 minutes | **Leveled Readers:** How Life Used to Be; What Was Life Like Before?; How Life Has Changed Over Time | Small Groups |
| **Activity 1** <br> Talk About the Topic | Discuss how historical topics (work, schools, etc.) have changed over time. | 30 minutes | **Blackline Master:** My Topic | Small Groups |
| **Activity 2** <br> Create a Timeline | Create a timeline of how a topic has changed over time. | 30 minutes | **Student Activity Mat:** 3B Timeline Magazines, butcher paper, construction paper, markers, crayons, tape, glue | Small Groups |
| **Activity 3** <br> Prepare Your Paragraph | Write a draft of an informational/ expository paragraph about the historical topic. | 30 minutes | **Blackline Master:** Prepare Your Paragraph | Small Groups |
| **STEP 3** ELL <br> Complete the Quest Write a Paragraph | Complete the informational/ expository paragraph about the historical topic. | 30 minutes | **Blackline Master:** Prepare Your Paragraph | Individuals |
| Deliver a Presentation | Read the informational/ expository paragraph to the class. | 30 minutes | Completed timelines, completed informational/ expository paragraphs | Whole Class |
| Answer the Compelling **Question** | Discuss the compelling question. | 15 minutes | | Whole Class |

© Pearson Education, Inc., All Rights Reserved

## Quick Activities

| | Description | Duration | Materials | Participants |
|---|---|---|---|---|
| **Compare Classrooms** | Compare and contrast classrooms from the past and present. | 10 minutes | **Blackline Master:** Classrooms: Past and Present | Small Groups |
| **Clothing: Past and Present** | Compare and contrast clothing from the past and present. | 30 minutes | **Student Activity Mat:** 4A Let's Talk/How Many? | Small Groups |
| **Past and Present** | Cut and paste items from the past and present into the proper columns. | 20 minutes | **Blackline Master:** Past and Present Scissors, glue, tape | Individuals |
| **Then and Now** ELL | Look at images of objects from the past and draw the present-day version. | 10 minutes | **Blackline Master:** Then and Now | Individuals |
| **Readers Theater:** Yard Sale | Perform a brief skit about two friends visiting a yard sale. | 30 minutes | **Blackline Master:** Yard Sale | Small Groups |

© Pearson Education, Inc., All Rights Reserved

# Writing Using Sources: Blast From the Past

**Compelling Question** ## What do you think about change?

Welcome to Quest 4, Blast From the Past. In this Quest, children will research how life was in the past, create a timeline, and then write an informational/expository paragraph comparing and contrasting how daily life (school, transportation, clothing, etc.) has changed from the past to the present. By learning about how their topic has changed over time, they will be prepared to discuss the compelling question at the end of this inquiry.

## Objectives

• Compare and contrast topics, including school, work, transportation, clothing, games, and holidays, and determine how they have changed over time.

• Create a timeline about the topic.

• Write an informational/expository paragraph comparing and contrasting our lives today with those from the past.

---

**STEP 1** Set the Stage  ⏲15 minutes

Begin the Quest by distributing the blackline master **Quest Kick Off**. It will bring the world of the Quest to life, introducing a story to interest children and a mission to motivate them.

> ### Story
>
> Your first-grade class has discovered a time machine that will allow you to travel into the past to see how everyday life was different and how it has changed since then.
>
> ............................................................
>
> ### Mission
>
> Step into the time machine to discover how some things—school, work, transportation, clothing, games, and holidays—have changed from the past to the present. By viewing the differences between then and now, we can better understand the everyday aspects of our lives.

© Pearson Education, Inc., All Rights Reserved

## STEP 2 Launch the Activities

The following three activities will help children prepare to write their informational/expository paragraph by researching their topic and creating a timeline. Note that all three can be done independently of the larger Quest. You may wish to assign the appropriate Leveled Reader for the chapter.

---

### Activity 1  Talk About the Topic  (30) minutes

**Materials:** Blackline Master My Topic

Display historical images of schools, work, transportation, clothing, games, and holiday celebrations from the Library Media Center or the Internet. Discuss with children how these topics have changed over time and how they compare with their lives today.

Then divide the class into small groups, and assign one of the following topics to each group: School, Work, Transportation, Clothing, Games, Holidays.

Begin by brainstorming with each group about what they know about each broad topic. Then work with children to narrow down the topic to a more specific topic of research. For example, children might focus on how chalkboards or books in schools have changed over time, how clothing has changed in sports from the past to the present, and so on.

Distribute blackline master **My Topic,** which contains questions that children should answer during their research. Have children write their initial answers on the blackline master.

---

### Activity 2  Create a Timeline  (30) minutes

**Materials:** Student Activity Mat 3B Timeline, Magazines, butcher paper, construction paper, markers, crayons, tape, glue

Explain to children that they will use the information they researched in the previous activity to create a timeline about their topic on butcher paper. Encourage children to include at least four points on the timeline. Potential points could be the founding of America, the use of machines, the invention of cars, or the beginning of the Internet.

Begin by explaining to children that a timeline helps them place important events about a topic in chronological order. If children need support, create a basic timeline on the board. The example timeline might include events from the school year to show chronological order. Then work with each group to place important events about their topic from the past and to the present.

Help children write important information, such as dates, names, or other facts, on Student Activity Mat 3B **Timeline**. Then have children create the timeline on the butcher paper. In addition, have children draw or cut and paste images from magazines or the Internet to add to their timelines.

---

**Materials:** Blackline Master Prepare Your Paragraph

After children have completed the first two activities, have them work in groups to prepare an informational/expository paragraph about their topic.

As children work on their paragraphs, tell them to review their answers from the completed blackline master **My Topic.**

Distribute the blackline master **Prepare Your Paragraph,** which contains sentence starters for children to use. Tell children to use the information they gathered during their research about their topic to complete the sentences.

## STEP 3 Complete the *Quest*

**Part 1** Write a Paragraph (30) minutes

**Materials:** Blackline Master Prepare Your Paragraph

After children have written the first draft of their paragraph using the blackline master **Prepare Your Paragraph,** work with them to revise and edit the paragraph for errors.

As children work on their paragraphs, encourage them to use this checklist:

• Did I describe what things were like in the past?
• Did I tell about how things are like today?
• Did I give an example of how things are similar?
• Did I give an example of how things are different?

### Support for English Language Learners

*Writing:* Some children may need assistance generating ideas as they write about how things were in the past and what they are today.

**Entering:** To help children generate ideas about how things were in the past and how they are today, act out the differences. Record details in a Venn diagram. Next to the diagram, write complete sentences using the details.

**Emerging:** Use a Venn diagram to help children generate ideas about how things were in the past and how they are today. Encourage children to begin their responses with *I think* or *I feel*. Write down their responses on the Venn diagram. Next to the diagram, have children write or dictate complete sentences using the ideas.

**Developing:** Model how to use a Venn diagram to generate ideas about how things were in the past and how they are today. Model how to formulate opinions with *I think* or *I feel* responses. Have children work in pairs to complete the activity.

**Expanding:** Model how to use a Venn diagram to generate ideas about how things were in the past and how they are today. Then have children complete the activity on their own.

**Bridging:** Provide children with a Venn diagram and explain that they will use the diagram to generate ideas about how things were in the past and how they are today.

© Pearson Education, Inc., All Rights Reserved

## Part 2 Deliver a Presentation (30) minutes

**Materials:** Completed timelines, completed informational paragraphs

Explain to children that they will have a Blast From the Past presentation.

Have groups take turns displaying the timelines they created. Each group member will then read aloud his or her informational/expository paragraph to the class. Tell children to point out the most important information on their timelines and to use the proper pace and tone when reading aloud their paragraph.

After each presentation, have audience members take turns using their listening skills to ask the presenters one clarifying question. Children will then answer the questions about their topic.

## Part 3 Answer the Compelling Question (15) minutes

After children have shared their timeline and read aloud their informational/expository paragraphs, encourage them to reflect on what they learned. As a class, discuss the compelling question for this Quest, "What do you think about change?"

Children have researched, created a timeline, and written an informational/expository paragraph about a topic that has changed from past to present. Encourage children to think about other topics they would like to research and learn more about, including how the topic has changed from the past to the present. They should use what they learned to answer the compelling question.

© Pearson Education, Inc., All Rights Reserved

# Blast From the Past

During a recent field trip, your class discovered a time machine. The time machine lets you go back and forth between the past and the present.

So how did people live in the past? What games did they play? What kind of clothes did people wear? How did they travel to school or visit their friends? You and your classmates will take trips in the time machine to learn about the past.

**Your Mission:**

You will travel back in time to learn how we lived in the past. Then you will write an informational paragraph about how our lives are different from the past and how they are the same.

© Pearson Education, Inc., All Rights Reserved

# To write an informational paragraph, do the following:

**Activity 1** **Talk About the Topic:**

Talk about how schools, work, transportation, clothing, games, and holiday celebrations have changed over time.

**Activity 2** **Create a Timeline:**

Create a timeline about a topic you researched.

**Activity 3** **Prepare Your Paragraph:**

Write an expository paragraph about the historical topic you chose.

## Complete Your Quest

Use your timeline and informational paragraph about your topic to present to the class.

© Pearson Education, Inc., All Rights Reserved

## My Topic

Answer the questions based on what you know.

Then research your topic. Use these questions to learn more about your topic.

Name of my topic: _____

**1.** What were things like in the past?

_____

_____

_____

**2.** How are things like today?

_____

_____

_____

© Pearson Education, Inc., All Rights Reserved

**3.** How are things similar?

_____

_____

**4.** How are things different?

_____

_____

© Pearson Education, Inc., All Rights Reserved

## Prepare Your Paragraph

Use the sentences below to help you draft an informational paragraph about your topic.

My topic is _____.

In the past _____.

Today, _____.

_____ is/are different

because _____.

_____ is/are the same

because _____.

© Pearson Education, Inc., All Rights Reserved

# Quick Activities

## Compare Classrooms

Small Groups ⏲ 10 minutes

**Materials:** Blackline Master Classrooms: Past and Present

Distribute blackline master **Classrooms: Past and Present.**
Explain to children that they will look at the two images of a classroom
and discuss how the classrooms are similar and different. Then point
out the word bank at the bottom of the page, and explain that these
words are items found in a classroom. Explain that children must
write down whether the item is found in a classroom from the past,
a classroom from the present, or both.

## Clothing: Past and Present

Small Groups ⏲ 30 minutes

**Materials:** Student Activity Mat 4A Let's Talk/How Many?

Organize children into small groups. Then have groups visit the Library
Media Center to research clothing from the past 100 years, such as
shoes, shirts, pants, dresses, and hats. Have groups discuss how
clothing has changed from the past to the present. Guide children to use
Student Activity Mat 4A **Let's Talk/How Many?** during their discussions.

© Pearson Education, Inc., All Rights Reserved

## Past and Present

**Materials:** Blackline Master Past and Present, scissors, glue, tape

Distribute blackline master **Past and Present.** Review the images that show work, clothing, games, and transportation from the past and present on the first page. Ask children to discuss what they see.

Explain to children that they will cut out the images from the first page and paste them in the correct columns marked "Past" and "Present" on the second page.

## Then and Now

Individuals ⏱10 minutes

**Materials:** Blackline Master Then and Now

Distribute blackline master **Then and Now.** Review the images on the blackline master and explain to children that the pictures show images from the past. Then tell them they will write a sentence and draw a picture of the same subject from the present.

### 🔵 Support for English Language Learners

*Writing:* Remind children to write sentences as they complete the activity. The activities here will help them practice their skill.

**Entering:** Ask children questions about different items they might use in the present, and have children answer using words or gestures. For example, ask: *Do you write with a pen? Do you listen to music on a radio?* Write down their responses in complete sentences. Then have children rewrite them on the blackline master.

**Emerging:** Ask children questions about different items they might use in the present, and have children answer orally. For example, ask: *Do you write with a pen? Do you listen to music on a radio?* Write down their responses in complete sentences. Have children read the sentences aloud, and then rewrite them on the blackline master.

**Developing:** Provide children with the following sentence frames to use to complete the activity: *I write with a/an _____. I listen to music on a/an _____.* Have them first say their complete sentences orally before writing them on the blackline master.

**Expanding:** In pairs, have children work together to write complete sentences. Encourage pairs to first say their complete sentences orally before writing them on the blackline master.

**Bridging:** Have children construct their own sentences about which items they use in the present. Have children share their sentences with a partner and discuss.

© Pearson Education, Inc., All Rights Reserved

# Readers Theater: Yard Sale

**Small Groups** (30) **minutes**

**Materials:** Blackline Master Yard Sale

Explain to children that in this Readers Theater they will be acting out a scene depicting two friends at a yard sale.

Distribute the blackline master **Yard Sale,** which contains the script for the Readers Theater. Point out the different roles, dialogue, and stage directions. If necessary, explain to children that dialogue is the words or lines spoken by the characters. Stage directions describe what is happening in the play that is not dialogue.

Organize children into small groups and assign a role to each child. Allow them time to read over the script and become familiar with the dialogue. Work with small groups of children as they practice reading aloud their parts. If necessary, provide support for any vocabulary children may be unfamiliar with.

Arrange the class in a semicircle facing an open area of the classroom. Then have groups perform their Readers Theater for the class. Tell children they should read with accuracy, appropriate rate, and expression. Audience members should listen quietly and not interrupt the performers.

© Pearson Education, Inc., All Rights Reserved

**73**

# Classrooms: Past and Present

Look at the two pictures below. One picture shows a classroom from the past and the other shows a classroom from today. Compare the classrooms. Write the words from the word bank under the correct picture.

| chalkboard | desks | smartboard |
|---|---|---|
| books | notebook | tablet |

**74**

© Pearson Education, Inc., All Rights Reserved

# Past and Present

Look at the pictures. Decide whether a picture shows something from the past or the present. Then cut and paste the picture in the correct column.

| Past | Present |
|------|---------|
|      |         |

© Pearson Education, Inc., All Rights Reserved

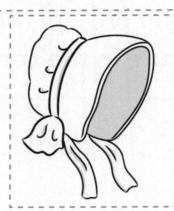

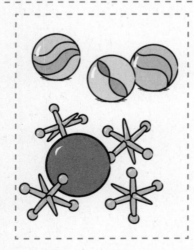

© Pearson Education, Inc., All Rights Reserved

Name _____ Date _____

## Then and Now

Look at the pictures on the left. Think about something similar that people do today.

Draw a picture of something today that is similar. Then write a sentence to describe your picture.

| | |
|---|---|
| Write a letter with pen and paper. | |
|  Visit friends using a wagon. | |
|  Listen to music on a record player. | |

© Pearson Education, Inc., All Rights Reserved

A story about two friends who visit a yard sale with a parent.

## The Parts

*4 players:*

- **Narrator**
- **Tony**
- **Alex**
- **Mr. Oaks**

*Director's Notes:*

*Set the stage as needed. The stage should include the following props (real or created) in a box: rotary phone, quill, and candle.*

**Narrator:** One day, Tony went to a yard sale down the street held by his friend Alex and his dad. A yard sale is when people sell things they do not want anymore.

**Tony:** Look at all this great stuff! What a cool bike!

© Pearson Education, Inc., All Rights Reserved

| | |
|---|---|
| **Narrator:** | Tony picks up an old phone from a far-off time: the 1980s. |
| **Tony:** *shakes phone and looks at it strangely* | What is this? |
| **Alex:** *looks at it puzzled* | Is it an alien? |
| **Mr. Oaks:** | It is called a rotary phone. |
| **Tony:** *looks at Alex confused* | It is a phone? How does it play music? |
| **Mr. Oaks:** | Rotary phones did not play music. A long time ago, people used phones just to talk to people. |
| **Tony:** | That is weird. |

© Pearson Education, Inc., All Rights Reserved

| | |
|---|---|
| **Narrator:** | Alex picks up a quill from a box. He turns it over in his hands, looking at it from all sides. |
| **Alex:** | Why would someone want to sell a feather? |
| **Mr. Oaks:** *smiles and shakes his head* | That is called a quill. People used to dip the end of the quill in ink in order to write. |
| **Tony:** | So it was like an old-fashioned pen? |
| **Mr. Oaks:** | That is right. |
| **Narrator:** | Alex picks up a candle out of a box. |
| **Mr. Oaks:** | That is a candle. |
| **Alex:** *rolls eyes* | I know what a candle is, Dad. |

© Pearson Education, Inc., All Rights Reserved

| | |
|---|---|
| **Mr. Oaks:** | In the past, people used candles to light up a room. Today, all you need to do is flip a switch. |
| **Tony:** | Or use a flashlight. |
| **Alex:** | Let us see what other cool things we can find! |
| **Narrator:** | Alex and Tony dug through the boxes. They found all sorts of interesting things at the yard sale, but no one was interested in buying the old items. |
| **Mr. Oaks:** *looking disappointed* | I guess no one wants to buy my useless old junk. |
| **Alex:** *suddenly getting an idea* | Maybe people just don't know how to use this stuff. |
| **Tony:** *nodding in agreement* | We can tell other people how to use this stuff; then maybe they will want to buy it! |

© Pearson Education, Inc., All Rights Reserved

**Narrator:** Tony and Alex go around to the other shoppers and explain how the items are still useful, just older. They compare the old phone, quill, and candle to a smartphone, a pen, and a flashlight and show how we can still use these old things.

© Pearson Education, Inc. All Rights Reserved

## Chapter 5

# One Nation, Many People

## Objectives

- Interview a family member about his or her culture.
- Read a story or other piece of literature from a different culture.
- Write a letter to a future first grader about their culture to place inside a time capsule.
- Create an artifact about their culture to place inside a time capsule.

| *Quest* **Project-Based Learning: Time Capsule!** | Description | Duration | Materials | Participants |
|---|---|---|---|---|
| **STEP 1**<br>Set the Stage | Read a blackline master as an introduction to the project. | 15 minutes | **Blackline Master:** Quest Kick Off | Whole Class |
| **STEP 2**<br>Launch the Activities | | 5 minutes | **Leveled Readers:** Sharing Our Culture; What Makes Our Culture Special?; A Time Capsule for the Future | Whole Class |
| **Activity 1**<br>Talk about Your Culture | Interview a family member about his or her culture and traditions. | 30 minutes | **Blackline Master:** Interview Questions | Individual |
| **Activity 2**<br>Read about a Culture | Read folk tales, folk songs, or legends from a culture. | 30 minutes | Books about specific cultures and traditions | Small Groups |
| **Activity 3**<br>Write a Letter | Write a letter to a future first grader about your culture. | 30 minutes | Completed **Blackline Master:** Interview Questions **Blackline Master:** My Letter | Individuals |
| **STEP 3** **ELL**<br>Complete the Quest<br>Create an Artifact | Create an artifact about their culture. | 60 minutes | scissors, construction paper, markers, crayons, tape, glue, cardboard | Individuals |
| Deliver a Presentation | Present their cultural artifacts to the class. | 30 minutes | **Blackline Master:** Prepare Your Presentation | Whole Class |
| Answer the **Compelling Question** | Discuss the compelling question. | 15 minutes | | Whole Class |

© Pearson Education, Inc., All Rights Reserved

## Quick Activities

| | Description | Duration | Materials | Participants |
|---|---|---|---|---|
| **Cultural Clothing** | Discuss the ceremonial outfits from different cultures. | 15 minutes | **Blackline Master:** Cultural Clothing | Small Groups |
| **Sacagawea** | Read about Sacagawea and research additional information about her. | 20 minutes | **Blackline Master:** Sacagawea, Library Media Center, Internet<br>**Student Activity Mat:** 1B United States Outline | Small Groups |
| **Tricksters** ELL | Read about the tricksters Anansi and Coyote. | 15 minutes | **Blackline Master:** Tricksters<br>**Blackline Master:** Anansi and Coyote | Small Groups |
| **Talk about Cultures** | Talk about the food, language, clothing, and other topics of cultures. | 15 minutes | **Student Activity Mat:** 4A Let's Talk/How Many? | Whole Class |
| **Read Aloud:** New Year's Traditions Around the World | Read about the New Year traditions of different cultures. | 15 minutes | **Blackline Master:** New Year's Traditions Around the World | Whole Class |

© Pearson Education, Inc., All Rights Reserved

# Project-Based Learning: Time Capsule!

**Compelling Question  How can we share our culture?**

Welcome to Quest 5, Time Capsule! In this Quest, children will interview a family member about their culture, read a story or other piece of literature from another culture, and then write a letter to a future first grader about what they learned about the culture. They will also create an artifact about their culture and place the artifact and letter into a time capsule. By learning about different cultures, they will be prepared to discuss the compelling question at the end of this inquiry.

## Objectives

- Interview a family member about their culture.
- Read a story or other piece of literature from a different culture.
- Write a letter to a future first grader about their culture to place inside a time capsule.
- Create an artifact about their culture to place inside a time capsule.

**STEP 1  Set the Stage  ⏱ 15 minutes**

Begin the Quest by distributing the blackline master **Quest Kick Off.** It will bring the world of the Quest to life, introducing a story to interest children and a mission to motivate them.

### Story

Your class is preparing a time capsule, which is a collection of items gathered today and then buried to be discovered by people in the future. A time capsule allows us to directly give items that represent us to people in the future. That way, they can better understand our time period.

### Mission

First, you will learn information about your own culture as well as different cultures. Then you will write letters and create artifacts to place in the time capsule. These items will be discovered by people in the future—as if we're speaking directly to them!

© Pearson Education, Inc., All Rights Reserved

# STEP 2 Launch the Activities

The following three activities will help children prepare for their cultural artifacts by researching and reading about their culture and writing letters to a future first grader. Note that all three can be done independently of the larger inquiry. You may wish to begin by assigning the appropriate Leveled Reader for the chapter.

## Activity 1 Talk about Your Culture (30) minutes

**Materials:** Blackline Master Interview Questions

Define the word *culture* and discuss with children. Explain that culture is the beliefs, customs, and traditions of a group of people. Ask children to discuss which different cultures they are familiar with, including their own. Then explain to children that they will interview someone in their family about their family's culture and traditions.

Distribute blackline master **Interview Questions,** which contains a list of interview questions. Children will ask a family member about their culture and traditions, including food, dress, stories, and so on. Have children ask the interview questions on the blackline master, and then write any additional interview questions they generate on their own. In addition, ask children to bring in any artifacts from their culture, such as photographs or other items, to share with the class.

## Activity 2 Read about a Culture (30) minutes

**Materials:** books about specific cultures and traditions

After children have interviewed a family member about their culture and traditions, divide the class into small groups. Then assign each group a culture based on the cultures represented in the classroom. Assign to each group stories, folk tales, folk songs, or legends to read from that culture.

Research stories, folk tales, and so on, from the Library Media Center, as well as from the following books:

- *Festivals & Folksongs Around the World* by John Higgins
- *Everybody Cooks Rice* by Norah Dooley
- *Whoever You Are* by Mem Fox
- *Jouanah: A Hmong Cinderella* by Jewell Reinhart Coburn and Tzexa Cherta Lee

Once children have read the material, they will then discuss what they learned about the culture and how it is similar to and different from their own culture.

© Pearson Education, Inc., All Rights Reserved

© Pearson Education, Inc., All Rights Reserved

**Activity 3** **Write a Letter**  **minutes**

**Materials:** Completed Blackline Master Interview Questions
Blackline Master My Letter

Have children return to the blackline master **Interview Questions** they filled out when they interviewed a family member in Activity 1. Have them reread the information they gathered about their family's culture and traditions.

Distribute blackline master **My Letter.** Tell children that they will write a letter to a future first grader based on what they learned about their cultural background during the interview. Explain that their letter will then be placed in the time capsule at the end of the Quest so that their culture and traditions can be preserved and shared with people in the future.

## STEP 3 Complete the *Quest*

**Part 1** **Create an Artifact**  **minutes**

**Materials:** scissors, construction paper, markers, crayons, tape, glue, cardboard, paper

After children have completed the activities above, have them create an artifact based on the information they gathered during the interview. If children are having trouble generating ideas about their artifact, provide examples such as recipes, illustrations of clothing or family members, maps or drawings of where their family is from, and so on. Explain to children that they will add these artifacts to the time capsule at the end of the Quest.

**Part 2** **Deliver a Presentation**  **minutes**

**Materials:** Blackline Master Prepare Your Presentation

Explain to children that they will have a cultural show-and-tell in which they will present their cultural artifacts to the class in the form of an oral presentation.

Distribute the blackline master **Prepare Your Presentation** for children to use as sentence starters for their presentations. For their presentation, children will answer the following questions:

• What is the artifact?

• What culture is the artifact from?

• Why is the artifact important?

After each presentation, have children in the audience take turns using their listening skills to ask the presenters one "clarifying" question. Presenters will then answer any questions about their cultural artifact.

Bring a large box into the classroom to serve as the time capsule. When children have competed their presentations, have them place their letters and artifacts inside. If possible, allow children to take turns bringing home the time capsule box to share with their families.

**ELL** ## Support for English Language Learners

*Writing:* Children will create a cultural artifact and present the artifact to the class. Some children may need assistance in their presentations.

Remind children to use their writing to clearly explain ideas and information about their cultural artifacts.

**Entering:** Ask children to share their artifact. Encourage them to use words and gestures to give more information about the artifact. Help children turn their responses into sentences.

**Emerging:** Ask children questions about their artifact and have them answer orally. Write their responses for them. Have children read the sentences aloud and then rewrite them for their artifact presentations.

**Developing:** Provide children with sentence frames to use to complete their artifact descriptions. Have them first say their complete sentences. Then help them write them.

**Expanding:** Provide children with sentence frames to use to complete their artifact descriptions. Have them first say their complete sentences before writing them.

**Bridging:** Have children construct their own sentences about their artifact. Children should say their sentences to you first before writing them.

---

**Part 3** **Answer the Compelling Question**  **minutes**

After groups have finished presenting their artifacts, encourage them to reflect on what they learned. As a class, discuss the compelling question for this Quest, "How can we share our culture?"

Children have learned about their culture and about many other cultures. Encourage children to think about any other cultures and traditions they would like to research. They should use what they learned to answer the compelling question.

© Pearson Education, Inc., All Rights Reserved

# Time Capsule!

News flash! The history museum has discovered a time capsule! When museum workers opened the time capsule, they discovered letters and artifacts from a first-grade class long ago. The letters and artifacts showed the different cultures and traditions of the past. Now the history museum wants your class to create its own time capsule.

Your mission: Your class is preparing a time capsule. Gather information about different cultures and create artifacts to place in the time capsule.

© Pearson Education, Inc., All Rights Reserved

# To create your time capsule, do the following:

**Activity 1** **Talk about Your Culture:** Talk to a family member about your culture and traditions.

**Activity 2** **Read about a Culture:** Read a story, folk tale, folk song, or legend from another culture.

**Activity 3** **Write a Letter:** Write a letter to first graders in the future about your family's culture and traditions.

## Complete Your Quest

Create an artifact about your culture, and place the artifact and letter inside a time capsule.

**90**

© Pearson Education, Inc., All Rights Reserved

# Activity 1

## Interview Questions

Learn more about your family's culture. Work with a family member to answer the questions.

_____

My culture: _____

**1.** What is my family member's name?

_____

_____

**2.** How is my family member related to me?

_____

_____

**3.** What country is my family from and how does it relate to my culture?

_____

_____

**4.** What kind of cultural foods does my family member eat?

_____

_____

© Pearson Education, Inc., All Rights Reserved

**5.** What was my family member's life like?

_____

- - - - - - - - - - - - - - - - - - - - -

_____

**6.** What games did my family member enjoy playing?

_____

- - - - - - - - - - - - - - - - - - - - -

_____

**7.** What legends or songs would my family member like to share?

- - - - - - - - - - - - - - - - - - - - -

_____

_____

**8.** _____

_____

**9.** _____

_____

**10.** _____

© Pearson Education, Inc., All Rights Reserved

## My Letter

Use the sentences below to write a letter about your family's culture.

Address _____

_____

Date _____

_____

Dear _____

_____

_____

_____

_____

_____

_____

Sincerely,

_____

_____

© Pearson Education, Inc., All Rights Reserved

 **Findings**

# Prepare Your Presentation

You have created an artifact about your culture. Now it is time to present your artifact and culture to the class. Use the sentences below to help you during your presentation.

Name of artifact: _____

My artifact is _____.

It is found _____.

My artifact is important because _____

_____

_____

_____.

© Pearson Education, Inc., All Rights Reserved

# Quick Activities

## Cultural Clothing
Small Groups (15) minutes

**Materials:** Blackline Master Cultural Clothing

Organize children into small groups. Distribute blackline master **Cultural Clothing** and explain that the blackline master is a fact sheet with information and images about three different types of outfits worn in different cultures.

Have groups discuss the three types of cultural outfits and describe how they are similar and different. Then have groups share their findings with the class.

## Sacagawea
Small Groups (20) minutes

**Materials:** Blackline Master Sacagawea, drawing materials (crayons, markers, etc.), Student Activity Mat 1B United States Outline

Organize children into small groups. Distribute blackline master **Sacagawea.** Have children read the information on the blackline master, and then discuss how she helped the Lewis and Clark Expedition.

Then have children research two additional facts about Sacagawea using the Library Media Center. During research time, have children identify the Lewis and Clark route and trace it on Student Activity Mat 1B **United States Outline.** Then have children identify where Sacagawea met Lewis and Clark (North Dakota).

When children are finished, have them draw and illustrate the coin on blackline master **Sacagawea** based on information they learned during the activity.

© Pearson Education, Inc., All Rights Reserved

# Tricksters

**Materials:** Blackline Master Tricksters
Blackline Master Anansi and Coyote

Explain to children that a trickster is a character in a story who plays tricks on other characters or disobeys rules. Usually the trickster character is very intelligent or has some secret knowledge to help play tricks on others.

Tell children that two famous trickster characters are Anansi from western Africa and Coyote from American Indian folk tales.

Organize children into small groups. Distribute blackline master **Tricksters** and have children read the two stories about Anansi and Coyote. Have groups discuss how the folk tales and characters are similar and different.

Then distribute blackline master **Anansi and Coyote.** Explain to children that these images are outlines of Anansi and Coyote. Have children decorate the two outlines based on information from the two stories.

## ELL Support for English Language Learners

*Reading:* During the **Tricksters** activity, children will read information about two different types of tricksters. Remind children to read closely to determine the meaning of the text.

**Entering:** Read aloud the text and have children repeat after you. Use pantomime or images to explain any vocabulary words with which children may be unfamiliar, and have children repeat the words and their meanings to you. If necessary, use words from the children's native language to help them determine the meaning of unfamiliar English words. Then ask children to describe the tricksters based on their actions.

**Emerging:** Read aloud the text. Use images to explain any vocabulary words with which children may be unfamiliar, and have children repeat the words and their meanings to you. Then ask children to describe the tricksters based on their actions.

**Developing:** Pair English language learners with native speakers. Have children read the text aloud together and encourage them to use their finger as they read. Help define any vocabulary words with which children may be unfamiliar. When children are finished, have them work together to describe the tricksters.

**Expanding:** Have pairs read the text aloud together. Help define any vocabulary words with which children may be unfamiliar. When children are finished, have them work together to describe the tricksters and summarize the text in their own words.

**Bridging:** Have children read aloud the text to you. Stop the children periodically and ask them to explain vocabulary words or other words or phrases with which they might be unfamiliar. When children are finished, have them describe the tricksters and summarize the text in their own words.

© Pearson Education, Inc., All Rights Reserved

# Talk about Cultures

**Materials:** Student Activity Mat 4A Let's Talk/How Many?

Write the following topics on the whiteboard or smartboard:

- Food

- Language

- Holidays

- Sports

- Clothing

- Music/dance

Ask children what cultures they are familiar with. Then ask them to name examples of each of the topics based on the cultures they discussed. Encourage children to write their responses on the whiteboard or smartboard. Then discuss with children how they experience different cultures in their everyday lives. You may wish to supply students with Student Activity Mat 4A **Let's Talk/How Many?** for the discussion.

© Pearson Education, Inc., All Rights Reserved

# Cultural Clothing

Read and talk about the different cultural outfits below.

### Japanese

### Mexican

### Indian

A kimono is a long, loose robe with wide sleeves.

An obi is a sash worn around the kimono.

The kimono is decorated in bright colors.

The traditional clothing of Mexico is usually made of wool, cotton, silk, agave, or bark.

A sombrero is a hat worn to protect the eyes from the sun.

A *Charro* costume is the typical dress of a Mexican horseman.

A sari is a long piece of cloth wrapped around the body.

The sari is decorated in bright colors.

© Pearson Education, Inc., All Rights Reserved

# Sacagawea

Read the Fun Fact about Sacagawea.
Use the Internet or books to find out
two more facts. Write the facts below.
Then draw and color the coins.

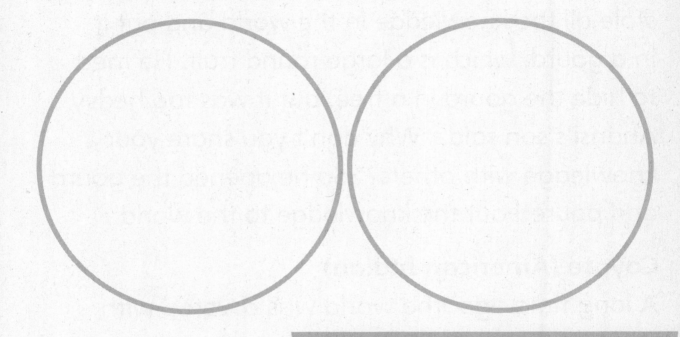

## Fun Fact
Sacagawea traveled with the Lewis and Clark
Expedition. She acted as a guide and helped
them explore western America.

© Pearson Education, Inc., All Rights Reserved

# Tricksters

Read the two folk tales about tricksters.

## Anansi (African)

Anansi was very clever but greedy. One day he stole all the knowledge in the world and put it in a gourd, which is a large round fruit. He tried to hide the gourd in a tree, but it was too heavy. Anansi's son said, "Why don't you share your knowledge with others?" So he opened the gourd and poured out the knowledge to the world.

## Coyote (American Indian)

A long time ago, the world was covered with ice. Only the pine trees high up in the mountains had fire. The humans and animals below were always very cold. Then one night, Coyote crept up the mountains while the pine trees were sleeping. He stole a burning stick and raced down the mountains. Before the pine trees could catch him, Coyote gave the burning stick to the humans. That was how humans discovered fire.

© Pearson Education, Inc. All Rights Reserved

## Anansi and Coyote

Color the pictures of Anansi and Coyote.

© Pearson Education, Inc., All Rights Reserved

# New Year's Traditions Around the World

People from different cultures have different ways to "ring" in the New Year.

Many Chinese people celebrate the New Year with big parades. The parades have dancers who perform a dragon dance. The dragon is a long float made of paper and cloth. During the dance, performers hold poles and raise them up and down to make the dragon move. The dragon is a symbol of wealth, long life, and luck. Chinese people set off firecrackers, too.

In Peru, one tradition is to place three potatoes under a chair. One potato is peeled completely, one is peeled halfway, and the other is not peeled at all. At the stroke of midnight, a person in the family closes his or her eyes and chooses a potato. A completely peeled potato means the person will have no money. A potato that is peeled halfway

© Pearson Education, Inc. All Rights Reserved

means the person will have a normal year. However, a potato that is not peeled at all means the person will be rich!

Rosh Hashanah is the Jewish New Year. It is celebrated in September. Rosh Hashanah is a time for a Jewish person to see how he or she can be a better person. During the holiday, a person eats apples dipped in honey. This is so he or she can have a sweet new year.

In Thailand, people celebrate the New Year with water. People spray and soak each other with water using hoses, water pistols, cups, buckets, and anything else they can find. Thai people also clean religious statues with water. They believe that the water will bring good luck and rain in the new year.

People around the world celebrate the New Year many different ways. How do you celebrate the New Year?

© Pearson Education, Inc., All Rights Reserved

## Objectives

- Identify the costs and benefits in stories.
- Create a character and plot to demonstrate knowledge of costs and benefits.
- Write a narrative that tells a story about a decision a character has to make and the cost of that decision.

### Quest  Writing Using Sources: Decision-Making

| | Description | Duration | Materials | Participants |
|---|---|---|---|---|
| **STEP 1**<br>Set the Stage | Read a blackline master as an introduction to the project. | 15 minutes | **Blackline Master:** Quest Kick Off | Whole Class |
| **STEP 2**<br>Launch the Activities | Watch a video with background information. | 5 minutes | **Video:** How do people get what they need?<br>**Leveled Readers:** How to Make Decisions; Weighing Costs and Benefits; Making the Best Decisions | Whole Class |
| **Activity 1**<br>Costs and Benefits | Identify costs and benefits in two common stories. | 45 minutes | **Blackline Master:** Costs and Benefits<br>**Student Activity Mat:** 4A Let's Talk/How Many? | Individuals |
| **Activity 2**<br>Create Your Character | Create a character using a graphic organizer. | 30 minutes | **Blackline Master:** Create Your Character | Individuals |
| **Activity 3**<br>Story Map | Create a story map to plan a narrative. | 30 minutes | **Blackline Master:** Story Map | Individuals |
| **STEP 3** ELL<br>Complete the Quest Writing Using Sources | Use story map and character sketch to write a narrative. | 30 minutes | **Blackline Masters:** Narrative Writing, Story Map, Create Your Character | Individuals |
| Answer the **Compelling Question** | Discuss the compelling question. | 15 minutes | | Small Groups |

© Pearson Education, Inc., All Rights Reserved

## Quick Activities

| | Description | Duration | Materials | Participants |
|---|---|---|---|---|
| **Transportation Maze** | Follow directions to "drive" a train and truck to different spots on a maze. | (15) minutes | **Blackline Master:** Transportation Maze, colored pencils | Individuals |
| **Play Store** | Pretend to pay for products with money within a budget. | (25) minutes | Paper, markers, two-column graphic organizer **Student Activity Mat:** 4A Let's Talk/How Many? | Small Groups |
| **Service Wall** ELL | Create a list of service jobs in the community for a word wall. | (15) minutes | | Whole Class |
| **Economics Word Search** | Locate hidden words related to economics on a word search. | (15) minutes | **Blackline Master:** Economic Word Search | Individuals |
| **Readers Theater:** Are You Done Yet? | Perform a brief skit about the costs of building a house. | (30) minutes | **Blackline Master:** Are You Done Yet? | Small Groups |

© Pearson Education, Inc., All Rights Reserved

# Writing Using Sources: Decision-Making

© Pearson Education, Inc., All Rights Reserved

**Compelling Question**

## How do you know if you have made a good decision?

Welcome to Quest 6, Decision-Making. In this Quest, children will learn about costs and benefits, and how weighing them is part of the decision-making process. Children will study the decisions characters made in fictional tales. Then, children will plan and write a narrative where a character makes a decision. They will gain the insight needed to help discuss the compelling question at the end of this inquiry.

### Objectives

- Identify the costs and benefits in stories.
- Create a character and plot to demonstrate knowledge of costs and benefits.
- Write a narrative that tells a story about a decision a character has to make and the cost of that decision.

## STEP 1  Set the Stage  ⏱ 15 minutes

Begin the Quest by distributing the blackline master **Quest Kick Off.** It will bring the world of the Quest to life, introducing a story to interest children and a mission to motivate them.

### Story

One of your classmates has plans to go to a movie with his big brother this afternoon. His brother doesn't come home from college very often, so he's really been looking forward to it for days. But your classmate just found out that his best friend got the newest video game that everyone wants. The best friend wants him to come right over and play the new game. Your classmate really wants to do both, but how can he do two things at the same time?

### Mission

Help your classmate decide what to do. Should he go to the movies with his brother or play a newly released video game with his best friend? Think about the costs and benefits. Then, write a narrative about a character who must decide between two things.

## STEP 2 Launch the Activities

The following three activities will help children prepare for their narrative writing by learning about costs and benefits and creating a story map. Note that all three can be done independently of the larger Quest.

Begin by showing the chapter video *How do people get what they need?*, which will give children the content background they need to complete the activities. You may also assign the appropriate Leveled Reader for the chapter.

Then divide children into small groups that will remain consistent for all the activities.

### Activity 1 — Costs and Benefits (45) minutes

**Materials:** Blackline Master Costs and Benefits, Student Activity Mat 4A Let's Talk/How Many?

Distribute the blackline master **Costs and Benefits,** which summarizes two common stories.

Explain a cost as something that is given up. Explain that a cost can be more than a monetary value. Provide an example. Then, explain a benefit as something that is gained or received. Provide an example. Inform children that they will identify the cost and benefit in each of the two common stories on the blackline master.

Depending on the reading level of children, read the stories aloud or have pairs take turns reading to each other. After reading, discuss stories as a whole class. Guide children to use Student Activity Mat 4A **Let's Talk/How Many?** during the discussion. Have children point out the cost and benefit of each character's decisions.

### Activity 2 — Create Your Character (30) minutes

**Materials:** Blackline Master Create Your Character

Distribute the blackline master **Create Your Character,** which has a graphic organizer to help children plan the two things the character wants.

Ask children to imagine a character for their story. Have children draw a picture of the character and include a name. Then, instruct children to think of two things this character wants. Model filling in the graphic organizer using one of the stories from the previous activity.

Have children complete the graphic organizer with the costs and benefits for their character's two wants.

© Pearson Education, Inc., All Rights Reserved

## Activity 3 | Story Map  ⏲ minutes

**Materials:** Blackline Master Story Map, Completed Blackline Master
    Create Your Character

Distribute the blackline master **Story Map,** which is a graphic organizer that guides children through the process of planning their narrative.

Remind children that they are writing narratives about a character who wants two things. Explain how the story map is a tool to help plan their story. Emphasize that the costs and benefits they created in Activity 2 will be the details in this activity.

Encourage children to follow the temporal words "First," "Next," and "Then." Once children have planned the sequence of events, point out that the story ending is the decision the character has to make. The ending goes in the last space on the blackline master.

© Pearson Education, Inc., All Rights Reserved

## STEP 3 Complete the Quest

**Part 1 Narrative Writing** (30) minutes

**Materials:** Blackline Master Narrative Writing, Completed Blackline Masters Story Map Create Your Character

Children use their completed character sketches and story maps to write their own narratives. Distribute the blackline master **Narrative Writing,** which gives children sentence starters to help guide the writing process. Children can illustrate their narratives to accompany the writing. If children are using the Realize course, encourage children to create their story using TikaTok.

---

**ELL Support for English Language Learners**

*Speaking:* Identifying and using temporal words helps children identify the sequence of events in a story.

**Entering:** Group children into pairs. Act out a sequence: eating dinner, brushing teeth, and then sleeping. Then provide pictures that show these same three steps in a sequence. Ask pairs to put the pictures in order and label them "First," "Next," and "Then."

**Emerging:** Group children into pairs. Provide each pair with paper with three horizontal boxes. Label the first box "First," the second "Next," and the third "Then." Give pairs three pictures: a child eating dinner, a child brushing his or her teeth in pajamas, and a child sleeping in bed. Ask pairs to put the pictures in order.

**Developing:** Group children into pairs. Provide each pair with paper and three horizontal boxes. Ask pairs to label the first box "First," the second "Next," and the third "Then." Give pairs three pictures: a child eating dinner, a child brushing his or her teeth in pajamas, and a child sleeping. Ask pairs to order the pictures and think of the sequence of events. Instruct them to tell a short story about the pictures using *first*, *next*, and *then*.

**Expanding:** Group children into pairs. Provide each pair with paper with three horizontal boxes. Ask pairs to label the first box "First," the second "Next," and the third "Then." Give pairs two pictures: a child eating dinner, and a child brushing his or her teeth in pajamas. Ask pairs to order the pictures, and draw the missing picture. Instruct them to tell a short story about the pictures using *first*, *next*, and *then*.

**Bridging:** Group children into pairs. Provide each pair with paper with three horizontal boxes. Ask pairs to label the first box "First," the second "Next," and the third "Then." Ask pairs to draw a picture for each box that tells a story about a bedtime routine. Have them tell a short story about the pictures to another pair using *first*, *next*, and *then*.

---

**Part 2 Answer the Compelling Question** (15) minutes

After children write their narrative, encourage them to reflect on what they learned. As a class, discuss the compelling question for this Quest, "How do you know if you made a good decision?" Children have learned about costs and benefits involved with making a decision. Encourage children to think about how a decision can impact others. They should use what they learned to answer the compelling question.

© Pearson Education, Inc., All Rights Reserved

## Decision-Making

One of your classmates is so excited to go to the movies with his big brother this afternoon. His brother has been away at college and he hasn't seen him in a long time. He has been looking forward to this for days. But your classmate just found out that his best friend has the newest video game that everyone wants. His best friend invited him to come over right away to play the new game. Your classmate really wants to do both, but how can he do two things at the same time?

**Your Mission:** Help your classmate decide what to do. Think about the costs and benefits. Then, write a narrative about a character who must decide between two things.

© Pearson Education, Inc., All Rights Reserved

# To write your narrative, do the following:

**Activity 1**   **Costs and Benefits:** Identify the costs and benefits in two stories.

**Activity 2**   **Create Your Character:** Create a character using a graphic organizer.

**Activity 3**   **Story Map:** Create a story map using a graphic organizer.

## Complete Your Quest

Write a narrative where a character has to make a decision between two things they want.

© Pearson Education, Inc., All Rights Reserved

## Costs and Benefits

Discuss the costs and benefits in each story.

### Little Red Hen

A little red hen, a dog, a pig, and a cow all lived on a farm. One day, Little Red Hen found a seed. She asked if anyone wanted to help make wheat for bread. The dog, the pig, and the cow made up excuses to not help plant the seed.

So, Little Red Hen worked very hard planting and watering the seed. After the wheat grew, she cut and prepared it for the miller to make flour. Little Red Hen used the flour to make bread.

Once the bread was ready, the delicious smell drifted through the farmyard. All the animals wanted to eat the bread. But since nobody helped her make the flour, she enjoyed her delicious bread with a nice cup of tea.

© Pearson Education, Inc., All Rights Reserved

# Ant and Grasshopper

In a garden lived an ant and a grasshopper who were very good friends. The grasshopper loved to have fun. He would play his fiddle all day while he watched his busy friend, the ant, work hard to collect and store food.

The grasshopper didn't understand why the ant was working so hard. One day he said, "Hey, Ant! Why don't you come and play with me?" The ant replied, "I cannot. I am storing food for the winter, when there won't be anything to eat!" The grasshopper laughed and continued playing his fiddle.

When winter came, the grasshopper could not find one single grain of food to eat and began to feel weak from not eating. The grasshopper saw how the hardworking ant had plenty of food to eat and he realized his foolishness for not storing food, too.

© Pearson Education, Inc., All Rights Reserved

Name _____ Date _____

# Create Your Character

Draw your character and think of two things the character wants.

© Pearson Education, Inc. All Rights Reserved

# My Character's Name: _____

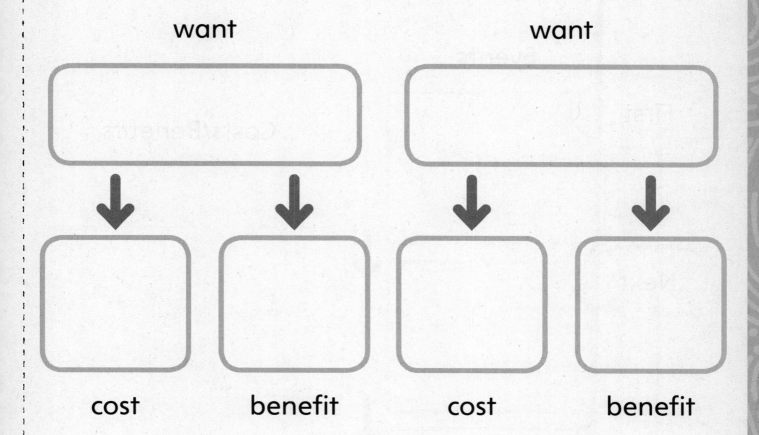

| want | want |
|------|------|
| cost | benefit | cost | benefit |

© Pearson Education, Inc., All Rights Reserved

## Story Map

Follow your teacher's directions to complete the story map.

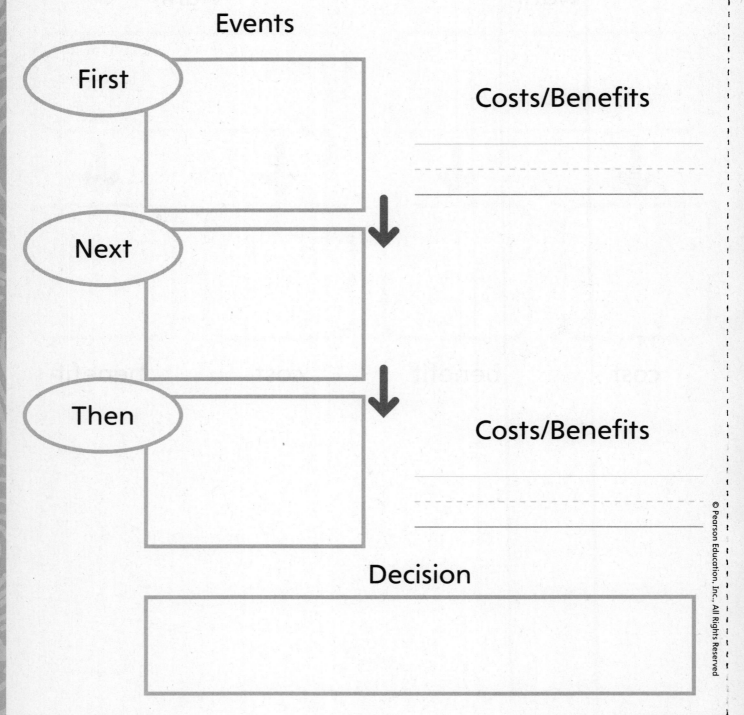

### Events

First

Next

Then

### Costs/Benefits

### Costs/Benefits

### Decision

© Pearson Education, Inc., All Rights Reserved

 **Findings**

# Narrative Writing

Use the completed Create Your Character and Story Map to fill in the blanks and write your narrative.

One day, (insert name of your character)

_____

_____ had a decision to make.

First, (character name) _____ wanted

_____.

Next, (character name) _____.

Then, (character name) _____ wanted

_____, too.

(Character Name) _____ could not have both things.

© Pearson Education, Inc., All Rights Reserved

If (character name) _____ chose (insert

one want) _____, then he/she would

(explain cost) _____ .

If (character name) _____ chose (insert the

other want) _____, then he/she

would (explain cost) _____ .

Finally, (character name) _____ decides

(insert decision) _____ .

**118**

© Pearson Education, Inc., All Rights Reserved

# Quick Activities

## Transportation Maze

**Individuals 15 minutes**

**Materials:** Blackline Master Transportation Maze; colored pencils

Distribute the blackline master **Transportation Maze,** which shows a maze of a town.

Instruct children to get out two different colored pencils. One color will be for the train stops and the other will be for the truck stops. Give children a series of stops for each.

**Train:**

- Take the train to the harbor.

- Take the train to the lumber yard.

- Take the train to the building store.

**Truck:**

- Take the truck to the building store.

- Take the truck to the house being built.

Allow children time to color in the specific places.

## Play Store

**Small Groups 25 minutes**

**Materials:** Paper, markers, two-column graphic organizer, Student Activity Mat 4A Let's Talk/How Many?

Guide children in making money that totals $50.

Gather items from the classroom. Give each item a price. Make copies of the two-column graphic organizer to use as a ledger during the exercise. Show children how to write their total amount of money at the top. Show them how to write each purchase and subtract how much money they have left as they shop.

Divide children into small groups. Model how some children will act as the shopkeepers and how others will be the consumers. Allow children to use their play money to "purchase" items. Use Student Activity Mat 4A **Let's Talk/How Many?** to create addition problems that relate to the purchases.

© Pearson Education, Inc., All Rights Reserved

## Service Wall

**Whole Class** (15) **minutes**

Explain to children that a service is a job someone does to help others. For example, a trash collector provides the service of removing trash. A homemaker takes care of the home and provides services to his or her family. A hairdresser or a crossing guard also perform services. Ask children to name the services a hairdresser and a crossing guard provide. Then, have children help you make a list of other services people perform in the neighborhood. Use the list to create a word wall.

**ELL** **Support for English Language Learners**

*Speaking:* Elaborating on language allows children to understand word meaning and context. Children will build off of their knowledge of services to describe services in order to expand nouns in simple ways. Model discussing homemakers and the services they perform. Explain that homemakers provide services to their families.

**Entering:** Have children draw a homemaker at work. As children share their drawings, say and list words to describe a homemaker. Have children echo you. Remind children that these types of words are called adjectives.

**Emerging:** Divide children into pairs. Ask them to list words to describe a homemaker. Remind children that these types of words are called adjectives. Then ask pairs to say a simple sentence about homemakers using one adjective.

**Developing:** Divide children into pairs. Ask them to list words to describe a homemaker. Remind children that these types of words are called adjectives. Encourage pairs to use an adjective that describes how the homemaker does the work. Then ask pairs to write a simple sentence about homemakers using one adjective.

**Expanding:** Divide children into pairs. Ask them to list words to describe a homemaker. Remind children that these types of words are called adjectives. Encourage pairs to use an adjective that describes how the homemaker does the work. Then ask pairs to write a simple sentence about homemakers using one adjective. Encourage pairs to write another simple sentence about homemakers using a different adjective.

**Bridging:** Divide children into pairs. Ask them to list words to describe a homemaker. Remind children that these types of words are called adjectives. Encourage pairs to think of many different adjectives. Then ask pairs to say a sentence about homemakers using at least two adjectives. Have the pair write down the sentence and share with another pair. If time permits, encourage pairs to say and write down another sentence using two different adjectives.

© Pearson Education, Inc., All Rights Reserved

# Economics Word Search

**Individuals** 15 minutes

**Materials:** Blackline Master Economic Word Search

Review each word with the class before starting.

- goods • services • manufacture • transport

- money • budget • cost • benefit

Allow children to give examples when applicable. Instruct children to find each of the words in the word search. The words are hidden horizontally and vertically.

© Pearson Education, Inc., All Rights Reserved

# Transportation Maze

Follow your teacher's directions to drive the train and the truck to different stops.

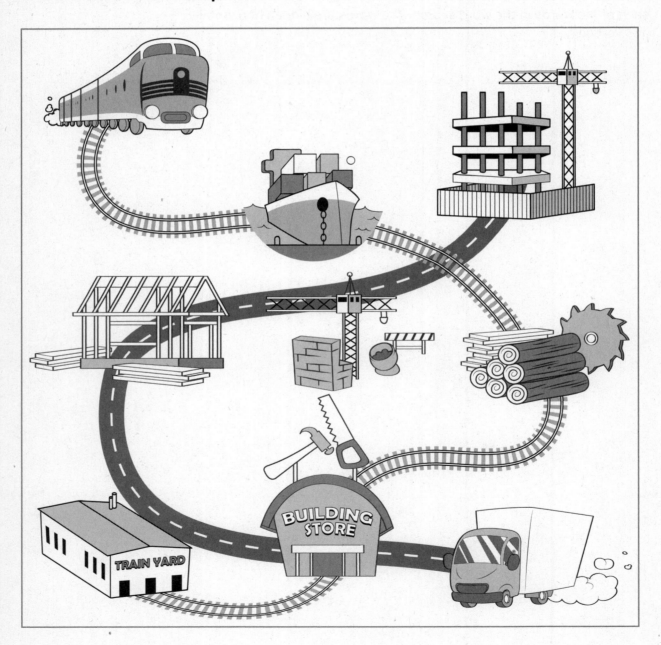

© Pearson Education, Inc., All Rights Reserved

# Economics Word Search

Find and circle the vocabulary words.

goods, services, manufacture, transport, money, budget, cost, benefit

```
G I E E C P E S O C E T
O E F S M O N E Y O H E
O P P I A R I Z E S R E
D T R A N S P O R T E I
S C T B U D G E T L V O
C E G T F N R B U S O B
A M E Y A C A F B E S E
N A Q A C A N H E A E N
U K C I T H K W R M R E
F N C Q U G I S T N F F
P G S E R V I C E S D I
S C O V E I I A D I S T
```

© Pearson Education, Inc., All Rights Reserved

**A play about a woman who is in a hurry to move into her new house.**

## The Parts

*5 players:*

- **Clarabelle** (woman)
- **Gus** (construction worker)
- **Maria** (store clerk)
- **Henry** (train engineer)
- **Harvey** (truck driver)

*Director's Notes:*

*Clarabelle is having a new house built. She is in a hurry to move into her new house. She continues to bother the construction worker, who needs to wait for the delivery of bricks.*

© Pearson Education, Inc., All Rights Reserved

**Clarabelle:**
*walking around nervously*

How long does it take to build a house? The Three Little Pigs had theirs built in a hurry.

**Gus:**

Ma'am, please have patience. We need the bricks to build.

**Clarabelle:**

Well, do not just stand there. GET ME THE BRICKS!!!

**Gus:**

It is not that easy, ma'am. The store is waiting on the delivery.

**Clarabelle:**
*dialing her phone*

Hello, Brick Depot? If your store sells bricks, then WHY do you not have any in stock right now?

**Maria:**
*answering phone at Brick Depot*

Hello! Sorry, ma'am. It is not that easy. The delivery was delayed.

© Pearson Education, Inc., All Rights Reserved

**Clarabelle:** Well, give me the number to the delivery service please.

**Maria:** It will not help, but the truck driver's name is Harvey. His number is 1-800-BUSY.

**Clarabelle:**
*dialing phone again*
Hello, Harvey? You are stopping the building of my house. Where are you and my bricks?

**Harvey:**
*answering phone*
Hello! Sorry, ma'am. It is not that easy. I am waiting for the train with the bricks. Then, I can drive them to Brick Depot. Would you like the train engineer's number? His name is Henry. His number is 1-800-RAIL.

© Pearson Education, Inc., All Rights Reserved

**Clarabelle:**
*dialing phone again*

Hello, Henry? Brick Depot is waiting for the truck driver's delivery. The truck driver is waiting for you to bring them from the brickmaker. Where are you?

**Henry:**
*answering phone*

Sorry, ma'am. It is not that easy. I had to wait for the bricks to be loaded onto my train. Then you will have to wait for us to load the bricks onto the truck. Then the truck driver will have to unload them at the store. Then the store can sell them to your construction worker. Then you can finally get your house built.

**Clarabelle:**

There are a lot of steps to get the building materials. I will have to be patient.

**All other characters except Clarabelle**

Yes, ma'am. Please be patient. THANK YOU!

© Pearson Education, Inc., All Rights Reserved

# K-W-L Chart

| What We Know | What We Want to Know | What We Learned |
|---|---|---|
|  |  |  |

© Pearson Education, Inc., All Rights Reserved

# Web

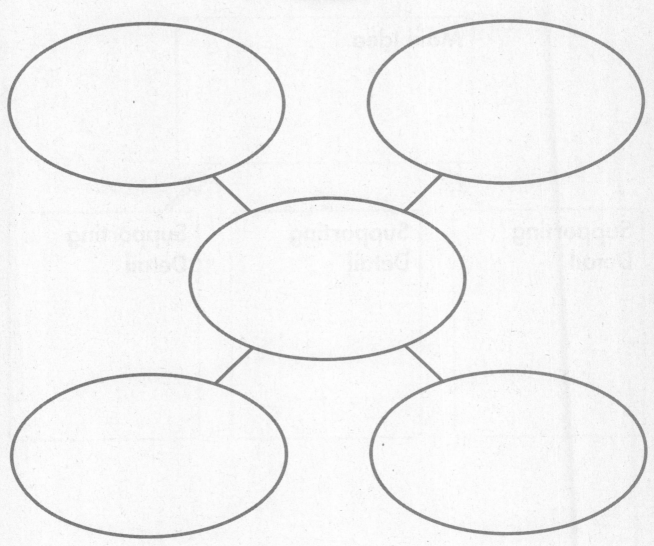

© Pearson Education, Inc., All Rights Reserved

# Main Idea and Details

| Main Idea |
|:----------|
|           |

| Supporting Detail | Supporting Detail | Supporting Detail |
|:------------------|:------------------|:------------------|
|                   |                   |                   |

© Pearson Education, Inc., All Rights Reserved

Name _____ Date _____

# Venn Diagram

© Pearson Education, Inc., All Rights Reserved

# Compare and Contrast

Topics

Alike

Different

© Pearson Education, Inc., All Rights Reserved

# Cause and Effect

| **Causes** | | **Effects** |
|---|---|---|

| **Why did it happen?** | → | **What happened?** |
|---|---|---|

| **Why did it happen?** | → | **What happened?** |
|---|---|---|

| **Why did it happen?** | → | **What happened?** |
|---|---|---|

© Pearson Education, Inc., All Rights Reserved

Name _____ Date _____

# Problem and Solution A

**Problem**

**Solution**

© Pearson Education, Inc., All Rights Reserved

# Problem and Solution B

**Problem**

‎ 

**How I Tried to Solve the Problem**

‎ 

**Solution**

© Pearson Education, Inc., All Rights Reserved

# Steps in a Process A

**Process**

..................................................................................................

..................................................................................................

> **Step 1**

> **Step 2**

> **Step 3**

© Pearson Education, Inc., All Rights Reserved

# Steps in a Process B

**Process**

..................................................................................................................

..................................................................................................................

```
┌──────────────────────────────────────────────┐
│                                                │
│  Step 1                                         │
│                                                │
│                                                │
└──────────────────────────────────────────────┘
                        ↓
┌──────────────────────────────────────────────┐
│                                                │
│  Step 2                                         │
│                                                │
│                                                │
└──────────────────────────────────────────────┘
                        ↓
┌──────────────────────────────────────────────┐
│                                                │
│  Step 3                                         │
│                                                │
│                                                │
└──────────────────────────────────────────────┘
                        ↓
┌──────────────────────────────────────────────┐
│                                                │
│  Step 4                                         │
│                                                │
│                                                │
└──────────────────────────────────────────────┘
```

© Pearson Education, Inc., All Rights Reserved

Name _____ Date _____

# T-Chart

|  |  |
|---|---|
|  |  |

© Pearson Education, Inc., All Rights Reserved

Name _____ Date _____

# Three-Column Chart

| | | |
|---|---|---|
| | | |

© Pearson Education, Inc., All Rights Reserved

# Four-Column Chart

| | | | |
|---|---|---|---|
| | | | |

© Pearson Education, Inc., All Rights Reserved

# Outline Form

## Title

..........................................................................................

..........................................................................................

**A.** ....................................................................................

    **1.** ..........................................................................

    **2.** ..........................................................................

    **3.** ..........................................................................

**B.** ....................................................................................

    **1.** ..........................................................................

    **2.** ..........................................................................

    **3.** ..........................................................................

**C.** ....................................................................................

    **1.** ..........................................................................

    **2.** ..........................................................................

    **3.** ..........................................................................

© Pearson Education, Inc., All Rights Reserved

# Answer Key

## Chapter 1

### Quick Activity: Fair or Unfair?, p. 12

1. Unfair
2. Fair
3. Unfair

## Chapter 2

No answers required for this chapter.

## Chapter 3

### Quick Activity: The Pledge of Allegiance, p. 55

I **promise** allegiance to the Flag of the United States of America, and to the Republic for which it stands, one **government** under God, indivisible, with **freedom** and **fairness** for all.

## Chapter 4

### Quick Activity: Classrooms: Past and Present, p. 74

**Past:** chalkboard, desks, books, notebook
**Present:** smartboard, desks, books, tablet

### Quick Activity: Past and Present, pp. 75–76

**Past:** transportation (person on wagon); clothing (bonnet); work (farmer plowing field with handheld plow, dressed in old clothes); games (marbles and jacks)
**Present:** transportation (person in car); clothing (t-shirt); work (person sitting behind computer); games (video game console and controller)

© Pearson Education, Inc., All Rights Reserved

## Chapter 5
No answers required for this chapter.

## Chapter 6
**Quick Activity: Economics Word Search, p. 123**

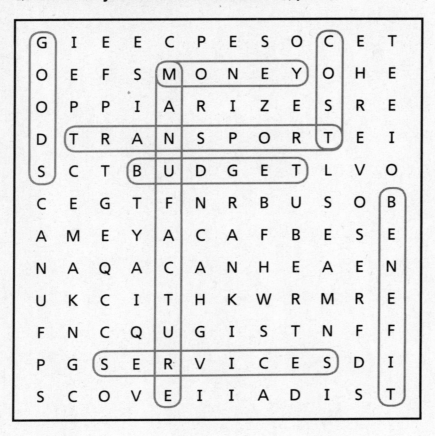

© Pearson Education, Inc., All Rights Reserved